Peter Chinyani

The Crooked Generation

Getting To Know Our Time And Our Generation.

Blessed Hope Publishing

Imprint

Any brand names and product names mentioned in this book are subject to trademark, brand or patent protection and are trademarks or registered trademarks of their respective holders. The use of brand names, product names, common names, trade names, product descriptions etc. even without a particular marking in this work is in no way to be construed to mean that such names may be regarded as unrestricted in respect of trademark and brand protection legislation and could thus be used by anyone.

Cover image: www.ingimage.com

Publisher:
Blessed Hope Publishing
is a trademark of
International Book Market Service Ltd., member of OmniScriptum Publishing Group
17 Meldrum Street, Beau Bassin 71504, Mauritius

Printed at: see last page
ISBN: 978-613-7-82345-3

Dedications

This book is dedicated to my five year old child Rechats Tinotenda Chinyani. I have always wanted to be an inspirational father, and I have put all the facts on how I can be that kind of a father to my child in this book. And through my child's life, I pray that many people may see the true reflection of how my wishful generation should grow and behave.

Acknowledgement

I would like to specially thank my mentor, the Apostle Dr. Gabriel Veyi. From the time I came to know him, he has never stopped to inspire me in the way he teaches and instruct. You are one of your kind in this generation. Thank you so much.

I do not forget to thank my better half Joyleen. She endured a number of lonely nights as I was busy working on this book. I know it was hard for her, but she was patient enough with me till I finished. Thank you my love.

I would also like to thank my Lecturers and co-students at World Harvest Theological College Johannesburg. Without your support and encouragement, I wouldn't have written this book. You are such a blessing. Thank you so much.

My special thank you goes as well to the leadership and members of Heirs of Promises Sanctuary Church in Johannesburg. It is through the support I got from this family that made this book possible. Thank you all.

My special thanks to the BLESSED HOPE PUBLISHING team. I found them when I was becoming hopeless of this project. And after communication with them, I found a positive respond from them, and at last my dream came true. Thank you so much.

TABLE OF CONTENTS

CHAPTER ONE

Introduction

Generations come and go, and each age bracket has its own challenges and troubles. The same in the generation we are living in today, but on the unfortunate, our age bracket is better identifiable as a **"crooked generation."**

A crooked generation is an age group that has missed its mark; religious values, cultural values, ethical values, etc. Most of these are emanating from the dysfunctional families, communities, politics and governing bodies. For every decision made in any board that is on the level of authority, it affects the whole practice and the world at large. The instability of the governing bodies causes serious implications upon the people pointed to it.

God created a man with true authority at the beginning. When a man lost his authority, confusion entered the world, and the results manifested even through his son who could not respect nor fear God anymore. The man used to live longer to above 900 years; but due to misconduct, and lost of fundamental values, the time limit has been reduced; and that is the sign of God's displeasure with the man's rebellion and disobedience.

The mediation of any lost generation is not within the power of a mere human being, it requires the supernatural intervention. An infidel may have knowledge and leadership qualities, but that cannot help to lead the people in the way God wants it to be. The nation of Egypt needed Joseph to interpret what God wanted; and the same happened in Babylon where God had to use Daniel to bring understanding to that kingdom.

Who then can serve this crooked generation from the direction it has found itself? Is there any remedy that can heal us from this catastrophe? If so, will we ever regain our position and authority as people? Does those who are leading, realize the danger in which they are putting us to be? The questions will go on and on, but the

1

answers are only in one a man, Jesus Christ the Son of the living God. If we can realize what Jesus did or can do in our lives, then we will know who we are, and what we are able of doing through Him.

May the Lord Help us see the dangers we are facing in this generation and direct us to do the right thing to save ourselves, and the people of our time. I pray that we do not see things and remain in our spiritual arena, but considerably stretch our spiritual eyes and see how we as the light bearers can help to save the future of our era. By saving the generation, I mean not to go beyond our limit, but to study and know what we need to do in such times like this. Some things which are happening now are part of the fulfillment of the word of God; so, nothing one can do to stop such. Yet we can help the people whom God has called and help them to persevere to the end.

This book can be divided into two sections; we will see in the first chapter the origin of the man, how God created him and the privileges, he had at the beginning. In the Second chapter, we will then get to know, how the man fell and how sin escalated into the world. In chapter three, we will then see the supremacy of the man's rebellion since the fall of the man to this present age. Chapter four will give us an idea of religious movements and how they are leading people astray. Whilst chapter five will then show us how cultures molds people's lives, and how this present generation no longer value it anymore.

The second half of this book tells us more of the time we are now living. It begins by giving clarity on the knowledge of time in chapter six. In chapter seven, it shows us how people are getting astray by seeking for miracles, signs and wonders instead of God the source. Then chapter eight gives us an understanding on how this age group is being carried away with music and entertainment. Chapter nine, finally gives us the solution to all the challenges the world is facing in our time.

CHAPTER TWO

Original State of the Man

"Then God said, 'Let Us make man in Our image, according to Our likeness; let them have dominion over the fish of the sea, over the birds of the air, and over every creeping thing that creeps on earth.'" (Genesis 1:26, NKJV)

When God created a man from the beginning, He created him with a purpose. Moreover, in His plan, He saw a man ruling the earth and everything in it. Upon creation, a man had authority, and God made sure that everything that is on earth submits to him. No created thing could do harm on a man, and nothing could intimidate him. He was perfect, without any blemish on him; all was okay with a man in his origin.

The problem began when the man decided to sin against God, it was then that he lost his authority and power. The created species, which were subject to him, could no longer do the same due to his position then. We will discuss more about sin, and what it did to the man in the next chapter, but here we will consider what the man looked like before he fell into sin.

The man was created perfect

The man in his origin was with excellence. God did not do a comparison with a man and other creation; the man was with the likeness of God Himself. He was highly exalted above any other creation that was on earth and none of them could compare to him. The man was an excellent being God had created because he could portray who God is. Let us have a look at what it means, '**to be created in the image of God**.'

"Human life was created in (lit., "as," meaning "in essence as") the image of God (v. 27). This image was imparted only to humans (2:7). "Image" (*selem*) is used figuratively here; for God does not have a human form. Being in God's image means that humans share, though imperfectly and finitely, in God's nature. That is, in His

3

communicable attributes (life, personality, truth, wisdom, love, holiness, justice), and so have the capacity for spiritual fellowship with Him." (**Bible Knowledge Commentary, 1983- 2000**) In fact, the man was originally God-like, with limitations. We will consider a few facts in respect to what was a man created after God's image.

1. In respect to his intelligence

God is the Supreme Mind. He is the Infinite Intelligence. A man is like Him, with mind and intelligence; he is capable of thinking. Moreover, the man's intelligence was the best in God's creation on earth. As much as the serpent being; 'more cunning than any beast of the field which the Lord God made'; It did not match the intelligence that was given to the man.

2. In respect to his moral nature

God created a man after His image, in righteousness and true holiness. With a benevolent disposition, God made him; with happy and prayerful spirit, and with a longing want to promote the general good of the universe. In this respect, he was like God, who is infinitely pure, divinely happy in His life, and in deep sympathy with all who are within the circle of His Being. In addition, everything around him, would love to be associated with him, because of how he conducted himself.

3. In respect to his dominion

God is the Supreme Ruler of all things in heaven and in earth. Both angels and man are His subjects. Material Nature is part of His realm and is under His authority. In this respect, the man is made in the image of God. He is the king of this world. The brute creation is subject to his sway. Material forces are largely under his command. Nothing under heavens can compare to Him. That is the dominion, which God had given to the man so that all things could be subdued under his dominion.

4

4. In respect to his immortality

God is eternal. The man partakes of the Divine immortality. The man, having commenced the race of being, will run toward a goal he can never reach. God, angels, and the man are the only immortalities of which we are cognizant. What an awful thing is life. We can clearly see how God had in mind in His creation of the man. He never wanted the man to die, but rather, live eternally.

5. In respect to the power of creatorship

A man has limits within him, but he has the power of creatorship. He can design new patterns of work. God gave him that ability; hence, we see many discoveries on earth due to the creatorship of the man. It is not amazing to see how the man are developing unthinkable things because they have that ability in them.

All of this is only to show us how God created a man in His original plan. God invested much in a man, for He wanted the best out of him. He intended for the best outcome from His creation, and all was to be in the fear of Him. He needed the man to follow His ways and do what was good for all the creation to learn harmony from him.

The man feared God

In his origin, the man feared the Lord. He knew his creator, and he was adhering to his precepts. He was a perfect example of creation in fearing God, and all creation on earth was learning from this wonderful being. The fear of the Lord made a man to keep the good relationship with God. Because a man feared God, it made Him to trust in God for everything he did. **To fear God, is to reverence Him, to do what He say, and live according to His precepts**. It is the inclination of God for His peoples to relevance Him. That will bring them closer to Him, and in return, He does whatever in His power to protect and keep them from the evil one.

The reason many people have fallen into the power of the evil is the fear of unknown. Moreover, once they are fallen into that trap, they have no choice but to do

5

what they are required to do. Unfortunately, the fear in which entangled them is not for the good, but rather leading to destruction. Nevertheless, it is rather good to have the fear of the Lord; since leads to righteousness with the results of good success.

Because the man feared God, he would spend much of his time fellowship with God. It then pleased God to have such a wonderful time to fellowship with His creation. God needs us, because He created us with His Spirit in us, so He wants to fellowship with us as we have His likeness within us. God would come now and then to have fellowship with the man, for no one on earth was suitable to have that deep intimacy with a man. Even today, if one is in a good relationship with God, they find themselves alone in their corner or secret places; and in that place the only person who can satisfy them; it is the presence of God. God loves fellowship with His creation, and nothing He is much pleased with than spending time with the man.

Fear commands respect, and everything or everyone you are afraid of, you are entitled to respect such. That was the case with a man, he feared God, and he respected God. He knew what God had said; he kept the command because he feared Him. The reason people should keep the commandments of God, it is because they fear Him. Once a people forsake the fear of the Lord, that generation is doomed for destruction. How can we expect a nation, or a people that leaves ungoverned by God to succeed in the land or world created by God? That is essentially impossible! Can one run a machine successfully without the original knowledge from the manufacturer? That will be complicated! God is the creator, so He deserves His due honor. **If people want to live successfully and have a life with full of days, the fear of the Lord is the key**.

It was the fear of the Lord that kept the man to keep going; as soon as the man shifted from the fear of the Lord that is when we saw him falling into the trap of the enemy. Many people today are falling into evil within a twinkling of an eye. Just a moment from where they are, they find themselves taken away into another world. **It is very important to guard our minds from the evil things of this world for the man has fallen with their intelligence within the twinkling of an eye.** Moreover,

6

how can we avoid that? Through making all the efforts to fear God, then Him will be able to keep His eyes on us and will protect us.

When the man feared God, even the creation that was surrounding him had the same fear towards him. All animals as fierce as they are, they were subject to a man, because he feared God and the power of God was upon him. When we fear God, He gives us a covering that makes other people to honor and respect us. It is amazing to see a man who wants his wife to respect and honor him, yet he does not subject to the highest authority. If one wants respect, he must learn to surrender first, and then honor will follow him. For as long as a man subjected himself to God, creation was subject to him. He had a special cover in return for his fear towards God, and any other creation around him could clearly see what God had done on him.

The man had a true reflection of God

In our days when a child is born and anyway a man is not satisfied with the baby, perhaps by the way how the baby looks; people are now opting for DNA tests. The reason they do that is for then to have an assurance if the child belongs to a man or to someone else. There is a general belief that, every child that is born must portray special features reflecting that the child belongs to the father. Part of those features, are physically seen, or at times, they can be indistinguishable through characters.

God created the man with an identification of Him. When we talk about a man created in the image of God, it does not necessarily point to the physical features. As I have alluded to that before it is not the physicality, which portrays God in the human being. God created the man spiritually in His likeness. **A man portrays God with the outcome of his deeds; the life of prayer, doing good, loving, and being merciful, and making the surrounding creation appear comfortable and live peacefully**. It is in these characters that we diagnose the godliness in a person, and it is in God's DNA to do such things.

Other creations can eat and drink just like the man; they can walk and see, they can communicate in their own world, just as a man do; but no animal have intelligence like the man. Intelligence was only imputed on the man not on any other creation, and the man should be proud of that. Unfortunately, due to misconduct the enemy infiltrated that intelligence and took superiority of the man's emotions to drive him off the goodness of God. When the enemy realized how effective the man was, and how was enabled to conquer the world; he decided to device a plan and make means to take him into destruction. It was now in the hands of the man to choose what was good and make the right decision, but instead he succumbed to the psyche of the enemy.

When God created a man, He intended him to conquer the world, and rule over every creature in it. Nothing and no one had that position, not even the angels. God had put the intelligence and His spirit of power in a man so that he can be able to rule just like Him. The earth is absolutely to the man's ruler-ship from the beginning, which means God gave man the right over His creation on this earth. He was to move in the power of God over creation and dominate the earth.

David considering the works of God in his psalm, he says:

> *"What is man that You are mindful of him, and the son of man that You visit him? For You have made him a little lower than the angels, and You have crowned him with glory and honor. You have made him to have dominion over the works of Your hands; You have put all things under his feet, all the sheep and oxen-even the beast of the field, the birds of the air and the fish of the sea that pass through the paths of the seas."* (Psalm 8:4-8, NKJV).

This only shows how much God values the work He did and the plan in mind as He created the man. He never created him anyhow, but He was so mindful of what He wanted to achieve through a man.

Even after the man sinned against God, as we shall see in the proceeding chapters, God did not give up on him. That is why even the death of a man, cannot be ignore lightly, instead whenever a man is killed; without a cause, his blood can still speak. The man is a complicated being; of which only God comprehend him fully. **A man was created a unique and awesome, and God did it knowing that the same creature, unique from any other creation, will glorify Him.** Not even angels were with advantages as the man! The man has a body, soul, and spirit; yet angels are spirit beings. It is into the form of a man that Christ had to appear with in this earth. Therefore, if God Himself could take the form of a man to come and save the world, it sends a picture of How God values such a creature. A man carries the image of God, moreover, God made him with His likeness, and accordingly he is unique and tremendous.

CHAPTER THEE

The fall of the Man and Its Consequences

"Then the LORD God took man and put him in the Garden of Eden to tend and keep it. And the LORD God commanded the man, saying, 'Of every tree of the garden you may freely eat; but of the tree of the knowledge of good and evil you shall not eat, for in the day that you eat of it you shall surely die.'" (Genesis 2:15-17, NKJV)

We have learned the original state of the man, how God clad him with power and authority over his creation here on earth. Now God gave the man the command as part of the stipulation to live well in His presence forever. God is ever authentic, and He is always fair in all He does. The man had autonomy over creation on which he would choose what to do with them whether good or evil. God did not impose on the man of what to do, rather He allows him to take his choice. It is in these regards God is ever just in His doing, for anyone can decide whether to live a life of pleasing Him, or can live as they wish. In return, God judges according to the choice a man make for himself.

God told the man that the entire trees in the garden he could freely eat, except the tree "of the knowledge good and the evil." With all the freedom of enjoying the entire garden, anyway the man was not content with it. He needed total supremacy of the garden, which was contrary to God's plan. With the inducement of the enemy, the man decided to munch the fruit, which God had forbidden them to eat. It is from that very moment that the man parted his ways with God. It did not have an effect only for him, but it corrupted the whole system of God's creation on earth.

The man disobeyed God

It is a dangerous thing to disobey God. According to my understanding, **the root cause of any sort of sin is disobedience**. If a man can obey the simple rules they are given, sin will reduce, and people can leave in harmony. It is a wreck of time to try to tell an individual to revolutionize his ways if his heart has determined to part ways with authorities. Once a person has made his mind to contravene, he then becomes dangerous in the society. When Saul propelled to destroy Amalekites, he was supposed to obliterate everything and everyone, but he decided to spare the king of the Amalekites, and fate animals. To that end, Samuel had no good news for him and he said to him:

> "Has the LORD as great delight in burnt offerings and sacrifices, as in obeying the voice of the LORD? Behold, to obey is better than sacrifice, and to heed than the fat of rams; for rebellion is as the sin of witchcraft, and stubbornness is as iniquity and idolatry. Because you have rejected the word of the LORD, He also has rejected you from being king." (1Samuel 15:22-23' NKJV)

We then learn that, **what pleases our eyes does not necessarily please God**. God does not need partial obedience, but unqualified. He requires us to do things according to His word, and nothing more or less.

Now when the man took the fruit to eat, he did not acquire the knowledge of good only, but the tree he ate, it was the tree of good and evil together in one. Therefore, in other words, of the same tree, the man would do the good, and would do evil as well. It is very unfortunate that, when the man was deceived, the devil did not tell him about the evil that would accompany their actions; rather he only told them about the good side. **I came to realize that, whatever said to us by the devil, whether good or evil, he remains the devil**. His intention is not to build you up, but to destroy you. Even if he comes and tells you your name, it matters not, what comes after your agreement it is not for the good. The very things the man knew entrapped them, and hence the world got into sin with a mere disobedience.

Because of the tree the man ate, sin came into the world that is when the man knew what is evil as well, what is good. After this knowledge, the man was left without choice but choose either to follow what is good or what is evil. In addition, whatever decision the man took from this point going forward it determined where every person would spend his or her eternity. That tree which they ate in the garden affected the entire world, and whoever was to come in this world was supposed to choose either to do what is good or what is evil. Thus, by choosing what is right, the man will then be on God's side; whilst by choosing evil, the man will be on the side of the evil one. Hence, from that moment, the man has decided to take his own course, God had no other choice, but rather to hide His face from the man's sight, for the bible says:

> "Behold, the LORD'S hand is not shortened, that it cannot serve; nor His ear heavy that He cannot hear. But your iniquities have separated you from your God; and your sins have hidden His face from you, so that he will not hear." (Isaiah 59:1-2, NKJV)

God does not associate with sin. Once a person takes a direction of living in sin, then God withdraws His presence from such a person. Sin stinks in God's nostrils. He is too holy to be in contact with a person who makes sin habitual.

Therefore, sin covered the spirit of the man, and God could not locate the man anymore due to sin. It is at that point that God asked the man saying, "Where are you?" (Gen. 3:9). Physically the man was in the garden, and God could see the physical part of the man, but not the spirit. David said, "Where can I go from your Spirit? Or where can I flee from your presence?" (Psalm 139:7, NKJV). There is nowhere a man can hide from God, but his spirit could not connect with God because of sin. God wanted the same fellowship He used to have with the man, but at this particular time, the man was nowhere to be located. **No matter how much good a person can be doing, on the very day when he decides to sell his soul to the devil, that person is cut from God's presence.**

Since the man was the first creation of the human race, what they did affected the whole humanity. Everyone who was born out of a man was then born in sin; because sin entered the blood and is transferred through blood. No one born out of a

12

man and woman can claim not to have sinned because it is in the blood. Even though God killed an animal to cover their sin for them to make their way back into God's presence; that could not completely remove their sin. Already, damage had occurred, and an overhaul was required for the man to have a proper life in God's presence. Hence, that is why God had to make a plan of restoration through His Son Jesus Christ, as we shall see in the last chapter of this book.

Escalation of sin

Now because of sin committed by the first man, we then see the results of it not too long from the day it was committed. Adam begot two sons and from these two we see the results figuratively shown. Abel naturally he was a good man, but Cain it implies he had evil in him. All that we see in Cain was never good. He had a rebellious spirit, which could not even recognize who God is; by his untoward behaviour, God warned of how the evil was creeping into his life (Gen. 4:6), but since he did not take heed of God's warning, he murdered his brother. It is at this point that we see what sin had done to humanity. Adam lived with animals for a time, and he could not do any harm to them, but here is a man, even though, they were no much people in the land he found himself killing his own brother. Whether he knew what he was doing or not, it matters less, but the fact that God warned and could not take heed of that, this is a sign that evil was already at work in the world.

Just a word of warning, **anger is one of the most dangerous things one should not entertain in their lives.** It is because of anger that Cain killed his brother; because of anger that many marriages are breaking; and most of the murders committed in the world they are anger driven. Our Lord Jesus spoke about anger in His teachings, and He compares it to murder. He said:

"You have heard that it was said to those of old, 'You shall not murder, and whoever murders will be in danger of the judgment.' But I say to you that whoever is angry with his brother without a cause shall be in danger of the judgment. And whoever says to his brother, 'Raca!' shall be in danger of the

council. But whosoever says, 'You fool!' shall be in danger of hell fire." (Matthew 5:21-22, NKJV)

The scenario Jesus is relating here is the same as what happened with Cain; Cain had killed his brother before he literally killed him. Murder is not committed when someone does the killing, unless it is by mistake, but it conceives and it nurture. All premeditated murder is committed before the actual killing. Once a person gets angry, and fails to control that anger, chances are high that the person may do something deplorable. That is why Apostle Paul said:

"Be angry, and do not sin: do not let the sun go down on your wrath, nor give place to the devil." (Eph. 4:26-27, NKJV)

So Cain could not control his anger because he gave the devil a liberty in him, hence he committed murder. This is to only show us how far sin had started to dominate in humanity, and that was just but the beginning of the potential harm of sin. There were no other ways of dealing with the harm at this point, as a saying in Zimbabwean proverb says, *"The dispensed water can not be obtained again."* It was difficult to turn back because the harm had occurred.

We then see that as the people were increasing, sin also increased on the face of the earth. The man used to live for so many years, to as much as more than 900 years, and they could see even up to the third or fourth generation of their posterity. Hence, as the number of people increased, the fear of God started to diminish, and that did not please God. Out of His displeasure, God decided to reduce the years of the humanity to 120 years saying,

"My Spirit shall not strive with man forever, for he is indeed flesh; yet his days shall be one hundred and twenty years." (Genesis 6:3, NKJV).

The wrong way of seeking God

Then God told Noah to build the ark, for He wanted to destroy the earth. God only reserved Noah and his three sons, and He had to start afresh with humanity. All

14

that was a way of reducing the level of sin, but nothing could do away with it permanently. This shows us what sin does once it grabs the human soul. Another Zimbabwean proverb says, *"What you are told to let go, is that in your hand; the one which is in your heart, you die with it."* Sin is not something one can test and easily get away with it. Apostle Gabriel Veyi always say, *"A man is not a sinner because he sinned; rather a man is a sinner because he is a sinner by nature."* Thus this beast called sin has to be thoroughly dealt with by all means. However, in as much as we can try to do it with our efforts it is impossible to win that battle, for it has something to do with life, and no one can save himself. We will then see in our next discussion, how the man can handle sin and find salvation.

After God had destroyed the earth and left a family of eight people, the man began their acts of disobedience again. People multiplied, and this time around, they now wanted to try to find God. They wanted to build the tower and try to reach heaven; their main purpose here was finding where God is. This is a problem with so many people today, they run around going into places to find where God is, but is God indeed in particular places, and not in other places?

Apostle Paul then tries to clarify the condition in which these people found themselves. As he addresses the people in Athens, he said to them:

"Therefore, the one whom you worship without knowing, Him I proclaim to you: God, who made the world and everything in it, since He is Lord of heaven and earth, does not dwell in temples made with hands. Nor is He worshiped with men's hands, as though He needed anything, since He gives to all life, breath, and all things. And He has made from one blood every nation of men to dwell on all the face of the earth; and has determined their pre-appointed times and the boundaries of their dwellings. So that they should seek the Lord, in the hope that they might grope for Him and find Him, though He is not far from each one of us; for in Him we live and move and have our being, as also some of your own poets have said, 'For we are also His offspring.' Therefore, since we are the offspring of God, we ought not to think that the Divine Nature
15

is like gold or silver or stone, something shaped by art and man's devising."
(Acts 17:23-29, NKJV)

Apostle Paul in this passage went all the way to show us what happen during the time when people decided to build the tower of Babel. In their mind, they thought of building and go to as far as God lives. They wanted to seek God with their own understanding, and in that way they even went far away from Him. God whom they tried to seek was not far from them, He was just where they were, right in their midst. It is not in the works of hands that God is found as some of other people's minds thinks. Most people have been confused by trying to create God's dwelling place in their minds, and they went to the extent of creating the picture of God in their own way. Yet surprisingly, God is none of those things they have conceived in their mind. The bible tells us that:

> *"But without faith it is impossible to please Him, for he who comes to God must believe that He is, and that He is a rewarder of those who diligently seek Him."* (Hebrew 11:6, NKJV)

We get to know God through faith, and by trying to imagine God with the human mind, many has gone astray. Some went to as far as finding the unthinkable things in a way of trying to prove whom God is like. It is out of that ignorance many ended up worshiping idols, some worshipped the gods whom they did not know. Moreover, even created their own gods, and they began to honor and worship the works of their hands, which does not speak, walk and not even see. Yet God the creator of heavens and earth, with all that is in them, He is not far from them.

It is out of ignorance that people do not comprehend the one and only God. If people can have the revelation knowledge about who God is, the world can be saved; but some have chosen not to seek for that knowledge, whilst some, their eyes have become blinded. The only source that can maintain the truth about who God is, it is His Word (the Bible), and nothing else. By trying to deny His Word, one denies God, because faith comes by hearing the word of God. **So if someone wants to know who**

God is, he must get to know His Word! Read the Bible, listening to good preachers, read good books about God, and in all this, one needs to avail his heart for instruction.

The confusion that took place at the tower of Babel was not necessarily for them not to reach where God is, but rather for them to fulfill the plan of God (which is to fill the earth); because that God whom they wanted apparently is not even where they were focusing on. A question has been asked, "If God is in heaven, where is that heaven?" **Heaven is a spiritual place where God resides, as of the location of heaven, one should not be too sure by pointing up saying that is the location of heaven**. The globe rotates, and if that be the case if where the sun is located be the location for heaven, how about during the night when the sun goes down? So being on the safe side, let us accept that where God is, that is heaven, or where Jesus is that is heaven.

If God had not perplexed this people, no one was going to stop them, they could have continue to build their kingdom and do nothing with God's plan. The same is also happening today, people are building their own kingdom, instead of building God's kingdom. You find out that people want to gather at one place, and they want to enjoy the fellowship, forgetting to take the gospel to the people outside the building. It was because of this same problem that persecutions had to take place in the early church, for the disciple were becoming comfortable to fellowship together instead of spreading the good news of Christ Jesus. May God help the church of today, to get out of its comfort zone, where they enjoy their fantasy, same language of communication, eating together, and power distribution; and go out to share the gospel, for that is the main purpose of the church's existence. How does it help, a minister and his church to have millions of dollars and do nothing to help in winning souls? Can we call that money a blessing? No! When the church got riches, soul winning should be one of the goals for that money. May God help us not to build our dynasts and our own kingdom but His, **Hallelujah**!

17

It was from the same place that nations emanate from, people then filled the entire world, and they started speaking different languages. As they went out into different places, God gave them different genetics to suit them according to the areas they were located. It was from that place, we find all kinds of people residing in different areas, which we now call **continents**. No one came from a special origin or nation of whatsoever. We all came from one place, but the only distinction is people as they went out, they discovered different things. And it is out of those discoveries that some began to subdue others and started to enslave them. Also in their discovery, some find different things of which some ended up worshiping their own findings.

So sin did not part with the man, instead as the world was being filled that's how sinning was also growing with the man, and the most dangerous sin that went on to dominate over the humanity it is **the sin of disobedient**. In those different places they find themselves in, they could not recognize who God is, even though He could speak to them in different ways. Some could ask for food in the bush and be supplied to them; in return, they would thank their ancestors. Some when they were in need they would call upon their dead, and once they get some help, they would say we better worship our dead people. In all this, God was not pleased, but He had to tolerate them to some extent, because it was a time of ignorance.

One may then ask a question, 'So what happen to such people who did not have the knowledge of God like we do?' Paul will answer to that and say:

"For as many as have sinned without law will also perish without law, and as many as have sinned in the law will be judged by the law (For not the hearers of the law are just in the sight of God, but the doers of the law will be justified; for when Gentiles, who do not have the law, by nature do the things in the law, these, although not having the law, are a law to themselves, who show the work of the law written in their hearts, their conscience also bearing witness, and between themselves their thoughts accusing or else excusing them) in the day when God will judge the secrets of men by Jesus Christ, according to my gospel." (Rom. 2:12-16, NKJV)

18

They knew God, but presumably they did not know how to reach Him, and seemingly the way to worship. By doing well, one would be saved by his deeds, and if one would not do what is right, then that means the person is condemned. Therefore trying to follow the way how those people worshipped or lived in the time we are living, will not make one to be justified. We now have the knowledge on how we should be worshiping and which is the way to God as we shall see in the following chapters.

And whatever those people did, it did not affect only them, but it has grown into a culture of which most people are now caught in it. It is for this reason that Paul told the church at Athens not to hold on to that ignorance. Our fathers knew not how to worship, they did not have understanding we have today. Trying to emulate how they lived without God, it does not justify our deeds. And it is in the same systems of traditions that the devil has taken his dwelling of which dreadful things are being done in the name of the culture and traditions.

The spread of sin did not only cause harm in the spirit of the man, but it has corrupted the good morals of humanity. Moreover, because of the lost of morality, the world has now experienced serious problems caused by bad moralities. At first people had lost the religious morals, but now it has gone to the extent of loosing even the cultural morals too. It is for this reason that we are going to see what are the effects of religious, and cultural moral lost is disastrous.

CHAPTER FOUR

Supremacy of Rebellion

"For rebellion is as the sin of witchcraft, and stubbornness is as iniquity and idolatry." (1Samuel 15: 23a)

The level of rebellious is alarmingly increasing in the entire world, regardless of the tribe or culture. The majority of people are fighting for power and this has led to rebellious in every walk of life. Woman no longer listen to their husbands, children can't recognize the authority of the parents anymore, communities takes the elderly people for granted, and the level of rebellion in the political arena has grown too ghastly.

The problem did not start now; it has been there for a long while ago. Since the man sinned against God, the spirit of rebellion has not left the human race. In many occasions, we have seen fights in different spheres of life, nations, tribes and even families. This is just but the results of what our forefathers did for us. In a nutshell, rebellious is a product of sin, and it can only be dealt with as sin and nothing else.

1. Children versus parents

The level of children rebelling against their parents has reached a startling echelon. Children are no longer recognizing the clout of their parents. They have reduced their parents to the level of their buddies. They found complacency in the name, but do not like to surrender to their authority. But is this what God intended for the families? Does God careless about the parents' honor by the children? Absolutely No! Something is definitely not right with the children of this age.

Honor of parents is one of the important things God values most. Failing to honor parents comes with serious repercussion. There are blessings and curses which come alongside honoring and dishonoring parents. Apostle Paul in his call to the churches, he made some emphasis on honoring parents and he said this:

"Children, obey your parents in the Lord, for this is right. Honour your father and mother, which is the first commandment with promise: that it may be well with you and live long on the earth." (Ephesians 6:1-3, NKJV)

Parents deserves their due honor, for they are the reason every one of us we are existing on this earth. God used them to bring all of us into existence on earth, and they were faithful to keep us until the day of birth. They played the serious role to nurture us and made all the possible efforts to bring us to maturity. They used a collection of resources to make sure that they raise us to be the people we are today. It is on this regard that failing to honor them brings a curse into our lives, for they will not converse well about us if we do not bestow them their proper honor.

This has been said in many Sunday school teachings, and some took heed of it. But it is unfortunate that not every child is getting the same information and understanding. Some attends Sunday school classes, not to get understanding, rather to please the parents. After that, none of the teachings will be applied; whilst some do not attend to those kinds of classes, doubtless because parents are not of the church culture.

This has affected our communities so badly, and it has gone even beyond our ability, such that trying to control the children has become a glitch. Children have taken their parents hostage and put them on an uncomfortable position. They have the fortitude to take their parents to courts for mere reprimanding. How then, can we expect harmony is such an environment? How can God be pleased with a generation that treats its parents like their peers? What manner of future is this generation heading to with this type of behavior and attitude?

This should not only be blamed on the children, but parents also have contributed to this cause. A small group of people in some parts of the world have agreed to sign for a move to allow kids to have rights, and within those rights, they gave them room to rebel against their parents. Parents were left with no choice but to live with that predicament, and they had to adjust, for them to be on the right side of the law. They supported the move unknowingly, and now the whole world is at risk of failing to control their children absolutely.

The preceding generations understood the principal of training up a child, but this generation has adopted the world's style of allowing misconduct. Hence, the world is loosing direction and the whole generation is at a risk of failing to fulfill its future mandate.

2. Young versus adults

There is a saying that goes, *"Charity begins at home."* Every good behavior starts at home, if children are not properly trained, it does not only affect their own home, but it will go down to the neighborhood and ultimately the nation at large. If parents fail to discipline their children, the domino effects are manifested in the way they relate to the elderly people in general. The same way they delicacy their parents in their own domicile, is the same way they will show off exterior. This then means, in whatever way a child behave peripheral, gives us a picture of their domicile. **Children are a product of their quarters; they portray a true picture of how things are under the roof.**

The misbehaviours we see in the streets, in the malls, in any gatherings, it is the upshot of how people infused in their quarters. We see young people who do not know how to deference the elderly people. In the past cohort, children used to stand for the elderly people to take a seat, but now they will snicker at an elderly person falling in the bus by loosing balance. They see an elderly person struggling to carry heavy stuff, they will giggle all the way and leave him to suffer. They meet a blind person beleaguered; they look and can even set a trap for him to fall. How can we expect delight in such an atmosphere?

If an elderly person rebukes the younger, they have the guts to tell him/her that, you are not my parent. In the past cohort, every elderly person was treated as a mother, father, grandmother, grandmother, regardless of where they originate. But in this age group, if you are not known, you are a stranger, and you have nothing to offer them. To aggravate the matter, some other parents are even condoning this type of behavior, and see it as customary. They will even go to the extent of telling their children that, 'you only pay attention to us as your parents, no one else.' How then can we build a harmonious state in such upbringing?

It is not normal for children to behave like misguided kids when parents are present in the society. The bible tells us that:

"Without counsel, plans go awry, but in the multitude of counselors they are established." (Prov. 15: 22).

It is not easy to determine high-quality effects with inadequate counsel. Where one fails, he must allow others to help and set up the good quality future of the youngster. A first-rate youngster must be applauded by the people of good behavior, not only the parents.

The cause of having crooked and irresponsible leaders in our society; it is because the families within the communities didn't heave leaders who would correspond to them with excellent attitudes and morals. We see the children being mischievous and we abscond them saying, they are not our children. Then at the end when we expect leaders, the same brood we did not restraint will turn out to be our leaders, and we cry foul. We saw them budding, and we did nothing to mold them, now we expect a miracle, at that old age? **It is not possible to straighten a crooked and bend sweet potato**. Once you find out that it is crooked (bent), you just have to accept it, or else you break it by trying to straighten it. The same applies to the age bracket we have created to ourselves. We either make them, or live with it for life if we can't work on them at an early age.

Institutions are there to help grooming the children, to nurture them in a way they suppose to grow. They need the support of the parents to execute their vocation. Children must be taught to respect every adult regardless of where they originate. Most of the teachers are no longer helpful in mounting the children for fear of victimization. Most of them (teachers) are parents, who are leading families, but some students have condensed them to the level of their brothers, sisters and buddies. They (teachers) no longer express themselves in the proper way of developing the future of our age group.

How I wish parents to help in bring back *ubuntu* in the people where the youngsters can treat every adult with due respect? This would not only help in harmonizing the population, but it would help in making a high-quality generation and form an immense future. The world needs people who have superior etiquette to lead and funnel it. And the society can play that significant role to up bring the leaders the world needs.

We have seen instances where leaders are behaving like children in the parliament where decisions affecting the nations are taken. That is a true reflection of how the public is failing to steer the youngsters into proper bearing. Will this generation ever be restored to the earlier order? It is my wish, but that sounds to be a peak hill to climb, because of the position we have deposited ourselves.

3. People versus their leaders

Nowadays, most nations are characterised by strikes and demonstrations in opposition to leaders and governments. People are no longer satisfied by what other people are doing. They no longer trust any person in the position of leadership due to their lack of proper representation. Tribes, clans, nations and regions are now fighting for their own autonomy and independence. The spirit of rebellion has grabbed the hearts of people and everybody needs to be recognized in the society. Churches are splitting, not because people have different views or visions, but people are power ravenous.

All people needs a leader and it is impossible to have leadership without people. The leaders have the mandate to fulfill their responsibilities, and people have the responsibility to support their leaders. But it is unfortunate that in our time, leaders has become like placeholders. They imply to be holding positions, yet the real job is being ignorantly done for failure. This does not mean they have not planned well;

instead other people in their inner circle are leading and forming a conspiracy behind their back.

All the splits we see be it in church, or in the political arena, they are all caused by people who are within the leadership circle. This is only to show us that, our enemy is not the people who are doing such; but the spirit of rebellion which is working in the lives of people. Jesus Christ our Lord was not betrayed by a person from outside, but the one among His twelve chosen disciples. That is how far the spirit of rebellion can produce.

The biggest problem in the world is that, it is being led by people with selfish ambition. And that apparatus has been created by the devil to suppress other people in the name of a leader. **The biblical leadership is of servant-hood, but today's leadership has become autocratic**. They want every person to behave as if they are in corporal training, where when you are told to jump, you don't ask why, instead, you ask, how high. Because of this leadership, leaders have made enemies of themselves with the people they are leading. Human beings are intellectual beings; they know when they are being used, and when they are being helped. Dr. Apostle Gabriel Veyi always says, "*Controlling another human being is like witchcraft.*" It is very true, for we were created the same and God did not give anyone the right to dominate over another human being; but to have dominion over animals and creatures. A person is not a leader by bossing around another person. A person is a leader because he leads people. **Leadership is not commanding and ordering, rather leadership is showing people how to do things.**

Fights and uproars are emanating from these kinds of leadership other people are portraying. Every leader in every sphere of life must bear in mind that, they are God's representatives. It is God who raises one, and put another down, (whether a good or a bad leader). Therefore, failure to lead people in the way God wants them to be led brings serious consequences, not only to the leader, but to the entire people under his leadership.

The leaders are failing their people, and they use money and influence to make their plans succeed. Once they reach that level, they will no longer listen to the voice of their people; they will no longer consider their outcry; and they will need nothing to do with their people. They will start to live in their own world where none of the people they are leading would reach, and all the cries become none and void to them. When people realize that they are distanced from their leaders, then they rebel against them. So in this case, it is the leaders who are causing people to rebel against them. Am I then justifying rebellious? Absolutely no!

Rebellious is never justifiable! Whether it is done for good or bad, God forbids that people should rebel against their leaders. God knows when the leaders' limit is, and in due time ultimately he will die or he will change for better. We as human beings we have our own way of seeing things and we can judge with human understanding, but they are genuine things we at times fail to comprehend. People at times tend to fight against God in the name of democracy, yet it is the same democracy that brought this generation where we are today. People need to understand the mind of God on various decisions when they are being made lest it affects the rest of people's future. Many nations are no longer Christian countries, rather social countries. They have pressed their leaders to sign the bills that affected their morals and hence the devil has been given the leeway to venture into all their systems.

It is the people that push their leaders to divert from the original plan of the nation to adopt positive principals that affects the whole population. There is but just a few dictatorial decisions that have been passed into constitution, without the approval of the public. When the nation fails, it fails with both the leaders and its people. When the church fails, it's not the pastor that fails the church, but the followers would have contributed, directly or indirectly. But now when this happens it is sad that the leader will be the culprit.

This is how far the spirit of rebellion has gone. It makes people to think of themselves, and they pull out of the equation when things go wrong. The leader is always left alone in the air, yet when the decision was passed, the followers participated. And the amusing part of it is, whenever progress is made, everyone rejoices even if they do not know the mechanism used to bring about the sensation.

Many leaders have become vulnerable in many institutions. Once people notice a malfunction, they start to withdraw from the leaders, even though they have been together with him in all the planning. This then brings many questions in my mind, 'do we still have loyalty in people?' The bible asked the similar question:

> *"Most men will proclaim each his own good, but who can find a faithful man?"* (Proverbs 20:6).

A faithful man does not go against their leader behind their back. A faithful man sticks to the core values or principles set. If people could rally behind their leaders in all spheres of life, we would have a great and successful generation with a wonderful future, but it is unfortunate that leaders and its people in most spheres in the entire world are at loggerheads. No one trusts each other, everyone is right, and can do better than the other, hence many divisions are mushrooming and the devil smiles all the way.

Rebellion comes from the devil himself; he is the mastermind of rebellion. He knows what human beings can do if they are united, therefore he will make sure that people fights and his joy will be fulfilled. He plants rebellious spirit in the family so that the family fails to fulfill its mandate.

The effects of rebellion

We have seen a number of male children being rebellious in the families, because the devil knows that they carry a seed that can make the world a better place, and he will make sure that he destroys the male children in families. It is not normal when you see your child leaving the good culture you taught him from the childhood and begin to follow various cultures contrary to your belief. It is an attack from the devil, and it has to be eliminated.

27

Rebellious comes with serious consequences. Some nations in the world are facing the consequences of rebellion. When people rebel against God, no one can mediate for them. Certain disasters we see or hear happening are as of a result of rebellion. God does not associate himself with people who are rebellious.

In the book of Numbers 16 the bible relates a story about a man who was called Korah. Korah caused people to rebel against the servant of God Moses. And in verse 21 we hear God saying to Moses,

"Separate yourselves from among this congregation, that I may consume them in a moment."

This shows us that God was not happy with Korah's behavior of rebellion. Even today, rebelling against authorities brings some serious disasters in people's lives. Many people are wondering how come things are not going well in their lives. My advice is, if you are doing everything well and you are sure of it, but nothing is working; then, check out your position with authorities. Check if you are not rebellious against your family, church leaders, your community leaders, or any other authorities that has something to do with your life. That could be the remedy of your problems because God hates rebellion.

CHAPTER FIVE

Religious Movements

"Then many false prophets will rise up and deceive many. And because lawlessness will abound, the love of many will grow cold. But he who endures to the end shall be saved. And this gospel of the kingdom will be will be preached in all the world as a witness to all the nations, and then the end will come." (Matthew 24:11-14)

The world has become too religious, and people have lost the test of true Christianity. There is much attenuation and people can no longer portray the life of Christ in them. They carry the name Christianity, yet in reality they portray the contrary. Christianity is a lifestyle, not a religion. Therefore, if one decides to be a Christian, true signs of Christianity must be pretentious.

Jesus in the passage given above was showing us of the generation that was to come, and it is interesting to note that we are living in that generation. Many prophets have come, and they are all proclaiming the name of the Lord Jesus. But does that qualify them to be true prophets? No! It is the fulfillment of the scriptures which we are clearly seeing with our naked eyes. As the number of so-called prophets is increasing, we are also seeing the increase of religious movements.

Since the time of the early church, there were so many religious movements, which came up to this day. It is interesting to note that, all these movements are counteracting to the Christian movement. The devil is doing all that he can to amuse the church of God. He knows the potential of the church, and how far it can go in developing and building people. If the church of God can have the full opportunity to show forth what it is capable of doing, the world will be a better place to live. But unfortunately, Jesus said it clearly that, "They are not of the world, just as I am not of the world." (John 17:16).

29

The church of Jesus is not of this world; therefore, it cannot go beyond its limits to change the whole system of this world. We can only do what we are given to do by our Lord Jesus Christ. So the main thing as the church of Christ we can do is to make-sure the message about our Master's kingdom is heard. But as we do that, many challenges awaits us on the way.

Not all are for God's kingdom

Not every movement that is fulfilling this mandate of God's kingdom; rather others do have their own agenda, which is to fulfill their master's duties. We are living in a time when people are doing all they can to make names for themselves. They do not care of the dangers it comes with; what they need is a name, and publicity. With the increase of technology, people are doing some juvenile things, easily predicable, and some people who assert to be educated are being fooled with such mere seduction. It is not because they are not able to detect perky things, it is because their eyes are blinded, and they can not see what is brewing.

The devil is using some financial provision to promote the counterfeit movements to mislead the people of God. The bible says:

"They went out from us, but they were not of us; for if hey had been of us, they would have continued with us; but they went out that they might be made manifest, that none of them were of us," (1John 2:19).

The devil is using people who were part of the church, people who even learned the principals of the church. They know the cries and woes of the Christians, and they take interest of that to destroy the church of God.

We are living in a time when people are easily twisting the scriptures for their benefits and lead people astray. They take time to study the bible, some they even attend bible colleges and get degrees. They are known as theologians, and that is for the sake of their benefits. They go to people who are ignorance of the word of God and manipulate them to make them believe their lies with a mere twisted scripture.

30

They teach heresy and do bogus miracles, to make the unknowledgeable people to believe them.

Cry my generation cry! For the people who are misleading you they are of the household of the devil. They do not care of what will happen in the future, for they know their ending. Who will save us from this crooked generation? The generation where money has become the death sentence of many people. The sufferings have caused many people to lose their faith, and turn to follow the dangerous ways of the wicked one.

Money in the name God

They create positions for themselves among the leaders of nations. They pretend to do well in the name of good people. Their money has blinded the leaders, the judicial and even the nations at large. Even if their actions can cause death, marriage break, or any other unacceptable things, they walk out free with their evil deeds. No one can raise their voices against him or her; for they (evildoers) will device a plan to kill you, in the name of, "**touch not the anointed**." Who shall deliver us from this kind of people? People who understand the language of death and sacrifice of other people, and they do not care about the suffering of their own people. People who are not afraid of giving things which themselves cannot eat; petrol, glass, and spraying of doom e.g.

Does the bible literally teach that people should do such? If so, why didn't Jesus' disciples of the early church did not do that? Indeed the judgment of these people should not be diminishing. May the Lord do justice to the ignorant people led into such things by these ruthless people who comes in the name of prophets?

I have seen people who lost their last saved money trying to find help in times of trouble. They go and see the so-called prophet, and only to enquire they get charged; for them to be prayed for they pay, and before they leave to go back home, they are cornered to buy anointing water, anointing oil or anointed material. Is that biblical? Did we ever saw that happening anywhere in the bible? Then how come

31

people are easily fooled with such stupidity? May God open the eyes of people to see how the devil has stolen their knowledge and exchange it for foolishness!

People should be knowledgeable to understand that, as far as the bible is concerned, none of those things the so-called prophets give them can save their live. What those people are doing is only to make them poor and lead them to destruction. I would not want to say all of them are becoming poor materially, No! But truth be told, whatever riches the devil gives you, it is not out of love. He only waits for the right time to strike, and normally his payment comes with a sacrifice. So once a person accepts the gifts that are connected to the devil, one should be careful to find himself in witchcraft, or Satanism.

One think we must know is, whatever the devil promises it comes with a condemnation on it. I always say, even if the devil comes and tell you your name, the fact that he is the devil, never accept that. I have seen many people when they go to see those prophets; they are called by names and are told their cellphone numbers and to them it is a miracle. What does one's cellphone number save him from a trouble? All these are the tricks the devil is using to lure people into his kingdom.

Many people they are afflicted, and they are under the power of the devil, instead of finding right solutions, they run into the pit of fire, where no one is able to deliver them. Who then shall deliver such people from that pit of fire which they have put themselves? What manner of power can rescue out of that den of lions? May God open the eyes of His people to see the signs of destruction ahead!

How can one explain that a woman goes to get help because of barrenness and only to find out that the solution is for the so-called the man of God to sleep with her? Did barrenness start today? Why then would people come to that point of desperation, such that they continue going down into the pity? They are not to blame, but rather the generation they are living in has missed its mark, and the devil has taken people captive. People have become too fragile, and they are easily taken away by little challenges.

The increase of Lawlessness

The lawlessness has increased, and people no longer care about any advice they can get from anyone. Whatsoever a person thinks of doing, they can easily do it in the name of freedom. It is what people call freedom, which is leading them to destruction. They asked for freedom, and the same freedom has become a trap to their death sentence. How can one help in such a scenario? At one point I tried to help a certain brother by reporting him to the church leaders for bad behavior, he was still young, with a potential of a good future; but what did I get? He threatened to sue me for "deformation of character". That is how bad the world has become.

People have become lovers of money, more than their own lives. A person can sacrifice to die for money and yet he leaves that money where he found it. The bible tells us that:

"For we brought nothing into this world, and it is certain we can carry nothing out." (1Timothy 6:7).

It is a fact that we need money, but not on the expense of our lives. Life is too precious to waste on material things.

This is how religious movements are growing; people are coming up with different ideas to make names for them. Thus, when they realize that it is not happening they start to build their own empires. They give themselves a position, which makes their followers to see them as an object of worship, not giving God His proper position. They make certain doctrines to suit them and indoctrinate their followers. Usually those doctrines are supposed to match with the actions of the founder. For example, if one wants to have many wives, then he can justify himself with certain scriptures, and make a doctrine out of that. It is unfortunate that most of these religious movements they are breaking away from the church, and all the people who do not have a deep understanding of the Word follow them.

These things did not affect only the church, but it has affected this generation at large. Some people have come to the point of not trusting going to church anymore. And some have found the lawlessness from such movements. Communities have accepted to live with what they know, and hence when challenges come, they fall into any seemingly helping hand available; whereby most of them become victims of the dark world.

The church has been robbed of its power by various divisions and rebellious. Governments no longer get good advisers, for they are not sure of which side to take. Arguments among these movements and the church of God has then caused mistrust in communities, hence people are now living their own lives. Telling a person about church it has become a mockery and people are distancing themselves from worshipping the true God. That is what the devil has done to drain strength from the church.

The Godly movement

It is a time when the church should take its position and fight against the worm that has entered the world. Every Christian should understand the time we are living in and begin to take their position. Our Lord Jesus gave us a great commission saying:

> *"Go therefore and make disciples of all nations, baptizing them in the name of the Father and the Son and the Holy Spirit, teaching them to observe all things that I have commanded you; and lo, I am with you always, even to the end of the age."* (Matthew 28:19-20, NKJV).

He did not say we must go and make members of the church; He did not send us to gather people in great numbers; neither did he tell us to win the whole world, No! He sends us to make disciples. Disciple who are true candidates of heaven, people who know their citizenship, people who know their Master, and people who can live with their Master's ordinances. People who do not compromise with truth, but they stand firm regardless of the challenges. Ministers should be the pioneers of this mandate. They should take responsibility to equip members to know the commands of the Lord. They must help disciples to be grounded and teach them the uncompromised truth.

Many people are going astray because they lack understanding of the word of God. If ministers can stand on their position and teach the truth, they will be set free. Our Lord said:

"If you abide in My word, you are My disciples indeed. And you shall know the truth, and the truth shall make you free." (John 8:31-32).

The truth does not only set a person free, but it brings people into the refining of being made free. Once a person gets into the freedom making process, he will be transformed to become like the mold, and that is Christ Himself. If the ministers do nothing, then the devil will always come and take away people from the church, and make them victims of destruction.

The word of God is a powerful weapon that can save people from this catastrophe. Every individual should endeavor to be knowledgeable with the word of God and be sure to live by it. No child is forever fed by the mother, at a certain point; the child should grow and be able to eat on their own. It is at this particular time that individual should be careful to know the types of food that makes them to be in good health, or else they suffer with sickness or die of poisonous foods.

A well-trained child will not eat what he or she should not eat, unless he has enough proof on how the food was prepared; with the help of parents. It is not every food that is meant for individuals. I like certain foods, which is a taboo to others. That does not mean I should blame them for that, it is not in their culture to eat such. Therefore, Christians should learn to take what is within their culture, not to try to eat what kills them. It is only Jesus Christ who saves! The bible tells us that, *".....for there is no other name under heaven given among men by which we must be saved."* (Acts 4:12b)

Therefore, any other religious movements that go against the name of Jesus, the teachings of Jesus, and the personality of Jesus Christ, they are not of God. For Jesus said;

"I am the way, the truth, and the life. No one comes to the Father except through me." (John 14:6).

The way to the Father is found in Him, not in any other names, not through ancestral spirits, not through the dead people, but only in Jesus. No truth is found in the human philosophy, no matter how educated they can be, the mind of a human being is just limited. We are given just a fraction of understanding, so the truth is not found in us. The only person who is and has the reality of truth is Jesus.

Life is always physically limited to humanity. Depending on the life one can choose to live, after this life we are living, there is another live. So one can choose to live forever with Jesus, who gives unlimited life and free of charge. Jesus is the life we need to live without sorrow, and without Him, life is miserable. Christianity is not a religion; instead it is the lifestyle; and that lifestyle it is of Christ Jesus. The fact that He is living, all those who trust in Him are living. Moreover, they will not die because He lives. Some other religions fade as time went by, but that is not with Christianity. Therefore, one should choose Jesus to live.

CHAPTER SIX

Cultural Effects

"Thus says the Lord: 'Stand in the ways and see, and ask for the old paths, where the good way is, and walk in it; Then you will find rest for your souls'. But they said, 'We will not walk in it.'" (Jeremiah 6:16, NKJV)

Culture is the characteristics and knowledge of a particular group of people, defined by everything from language, religion, cuisine, social habits, music and arts. Many countries are largely populated by immigrants, and the culture is influenced by the many groups of people that now make up the country. This is also a part of growth. As the countries grow, so does its cultural diversity. And it is very important for people to understand how elderly people treated certain issues and learn to do what is right, because as generations comes and go, people have a tendency of missing the mark.

Culture influences the majority of the people in the community on how they should behave and also on how they should grow. Children from birth up to the age of five they are form by what they see and hear during that course of time. It takes God's grace to change and reprogram whatever that has been planted inside a person as they grew-up. A proper foundation should be made as the child grows, for it is the same foundation that will influence what the child will be and how he will behave. Many people have failed their children due to how they treated them whilst they were young, and as a result, they can not control them anymore even though they put some efforts. The bible says,

"Train a child in the way he [should] go; and, even when old, he will not swerve from it." (Prov. 22:6, Complete Jewish Bible).

Cultures, that influences the world

We have about five major cultures that influence our communities and each has its effects, and affects our daily lives, directly and indirectly. To some it will be for their advantages, whilst to others it would be a detriment. **Live Science** gives us a good explanation about; the cultures and how they originate.

1. Western culture

The term "Western culture" has come to define the culture of European countries as well as those whom European immigration has heavily influenced, such as the States, according to *Khan University*. Western culture has its roots in the Classical Period of the Greco-Roman era and the rise of Christianity in the 14th century.

Other drivers of Western culture include Latin, Celtic, Germanic and Hellenic ethnic and linguistic groups. Today, the influences of Western culture can be seen essentially in every country of the world. (https://www.livescience.com/21478-what-is-culture-definition-of-culture.html)

2. Eastern culture

Eastern culture generally refers to the societal norms of countries in Far East Asia (including China, Japan, Vietnam, North Korea and South Korea) and the Indian subcontinent. Like the West, Eastern culture was heavily influenced by religion during its early development, but it was also heavily influenced by the growth and harvesting of rice, according to the book *"Pathways to Asian Civilizations: Tracing the Origins and Spread of Rice and Rice Cultures"* by Dorian Q. Fuller. In general, in Eastern culture there is less of a distinction between secular society and religious philosophy than there is in the West. (ibid)

3. Latin culture

Many of the Spanish-speaking nations considerably are part of the Latin culture, while the geographic region is widespread. Latin America is typically defined as those parts of the Central America, South America and Mexico where Spanish or Portuguese are the dominant languages. Originally, the term "Latin America" was used by French geographers to differentiate between Anglo and Romance (Latin-based) languages, according to the University of Texas. While Spain and Portugal are on the European continent, they are considered the key influencers of what is known as Latin culture, which denotes people using languages derived from Latin, also known as Romance languages. (ibid)

4. Middle Eastern culture

The countries of the Middle East have some but not all things in common. This is not a surprise, since the areas consists of roughly 20 countries, according to PBS. The Arabic language is one thing that is common throughout the region; but, the wide variety of dialect can sometimes make communication difficult. Religion is another cultural section that the countries of the Middle East have in common. The Middle East is the birthplace of Judaism, Christianity and Islam. (ibid)

5. African culture

Africa is home to a number of tribes, ethnic and social groups. One of the key features of this culture is the large number of ethnic groups throughout the 54 countries on the continent. Nigeria alone has more than 300 tribes, for example.

Africa is divided into two cultural groups: North Africa and Sub-Saharan Africa. This is because Northwest Africa has strong ties to Middle East, while Sub-Africa shares historical, physical and social characteristics that are very different from North Africa, according to the *University of Colorado*. The harsh environment has been a large component in the development of Sub-Saharan Africa culture, as they are a number of languages, cuisines, art and musical styles that have sprung up among the far-flung populations. (ibid)

Now due to the increasing migration in the world, many people from different nations and cultures have mixed-up. As a result, cultures are compromised, and people can not stick to their original cultures anymore. No matter what culture a people are part of, one thing is for certain, it will change. Culture turns up to have become key in our interconnected world, which is made up of so many ethnically diverse societies, but also riddled by conflicts associated with religion, ethnicity, ethical beliefs, and, essentially, the elements which make up culture. But culture is no longer fixed if it ever was.

Culture in the Bible times

Abraham when God called him, he had a certain culture in which he grew up in, but as God called him, he had no choice but to change his culture. God had to reprogram him to match the new life he was to start living. The same happen to the children of Israel, when they went to Egypt, they had a certain culture, but due to the environment they found themselves in, they changed with time, and someday they became like Egyptians. This makes it difficult to define any culture in only one way. To some it is for the good whilst to some it is for the bad. We will try to see the advantages and disadvantages of changing cultures.

It is also very sad to note that culture was supposed to be good, but the devil took his hiding within it. Through mixed cultures, people have lost the actual value, and they no longer tolerate authorities, they do not value the parents and they lost their *"ubuntu,"* (sense of humor) because of the infiltration. This has not only affected the Christian community, but rather the world at large. Some have blamed it on the church through the missionaries who came to minister in their regions, saying they are the one who brought all the trouble they have today.

Jesus Christ in His conversation with the woman of Samaria in John chapter 4, he gives us an idea of how cultures affects our lives. He gives us a clear picture of how Samaritans were worshiping, and how they were affected by what surrounded them. Samaritans are the children of Israel, just like the Jews, but they part ways to the extent that they do not eat together with the Jews due to cultural changes. Samaritans when they were taken to captive by Assyrians, they were then mixed with other tribes which did not worship the living God. Because of that, they also found themselves involved in such kinds of worship, and they intermarried with other tribes who were not of Israel. Moreover, because of these actions, they lost their original cultures and values. Hence, they did not know how to worship the true God whom their fathers worshipped.

And Jesus in His conversation with the woman, He is then pointing to the woman of their ignorance of worship. Jews on the other side they were religious even though they didn't understand the change that was taking place. According to them salvation is theirs because Jesus who is the Messiah came through the tribe of Judah. In these two kinds of worship, we will have an understanding of how culture and religion can lead people astray.

Culture in our times

The same challenge faced by other generations applies to us in our generation too, we learned certain morals and we understood its values. And among which, it is the way of worship, even though to some in a wrongly manner. We managed to keep those values to some extent, and it helped us to reach were we are today. But now the most important thing is to know the time we are living in, and the types of cultures we should be embracing that can advance us morally and spiritually. Unfortunately, people are now much concerned about dignity, rather than morals. Money has become loud speaking than fundamental values. Authorities can not speak, because money is louder than their words, what they do is to compromise their authority due to wealth.

The world has gone out of hand due to greed leaders, who do not want to stand on their real position and protect the good morals and behaviors. They have allowed the other cultures, which we cannot legitimately confirm, its origin, to influence the people. Moreover, by so doing, the devil has taken his dwelling in the nations through the people in a position of power. **Children no longer listen to their parents in the name of child abuse. Justice can't be implemented freely in the name of democracy and marriage lost its values in the name of gender balance**. May God help us to realize where the world is going! Who shall deliver this world from this crooked generation?

We are now living in a time when children's voices are heard better, than the parents' voices. The devil is stealing the authority of the parents hiding in freedom of speech and association, through the children. The problem has run out of government's control, as all the legislation are infiltrated by the enemy who intends to destroy nations from the ground roots, (the families).

Example of good cultures

There are certain cultures, regardless of its origin worthy embracing, and they bring stability and harmony in both the community and families. The **Confucianism** has certain beliefs worthy emulating. They have five great relationships which serve as a model for individuals' daily behavior. Jessica LT Devega& Christine Ortega Guarkee gives us an overview of these relationships, and they wrote:

"The five central relationships are *father-son, elder brother-younger brother, husband-wife, old-young, and ruler-subject.* Loyalty is a key theme that is present in all five of these important relationships."

(a) The *father-son* relationship refers to the parents' responsibility to instill moral values in a child, and in return, the child should be respectful and obedient.

(b) The *elder brother-younger brother* relationship points out the need for the elder sibling to help guide the younger one through life as an extension of the parents. The elder son traditionally inherits all the paternal responsibility.

(c) The *husband-wife* relationship is about mutual care, but the husband still has authority over the wife. He has to be the financial provider and protector while she is to be the homemaker.

(d) The *old-young* relationship (sometime even thought to be a *friend-friend* relationship) intends to foster loyalty and respect. The older person helps the younger in personal development and the younger cares for the older as he or she ages.

(e) Finally, the *ruler-subject* relationship is a reflection of the social order both domestically and within the larger society. The ruler should protect and care for the subjects, but in return, the subject should be obedient to and supportive of the ruler. (**All you want to know but didn't think you could ask, Struik Christian Book, 2012, p.120**)

Every individual can easily understand these general moral values because from birth it is the responsibility for every parent to teach children such things. But due to the dysfunctional families, children no longer have any of these moral. Schools used to help by molding moral values in children, but with some rules implemented in schools the teachers can no longer help; instead, they just look as the children are heading for destruction.

All those uncalled for rules and regulations emanate from the devil himself to bring confusion and lake of discipline in the children, hence at last they become useless and unhelpful. In addition, one of the disheartening things is, the governments are quick to conclude in such issues, especially if the agendas purposed by so-called powerhouse nations.

After all, when they realize such principals are in motion within educational institutions, those in power will then send their children to well managed schools that are with good moral disciplines; whilst other people's children are studying to suffer and fail in their own nations. Some other religions like Moslems; they made sure that their children are guarded against such principles by diffusing every negative thought given to their children everyday after school. They make-sure all their kids goes to a training place after school, where they teach them the moral values from Koran, and that is to keep good behavior in children's minds. Unfortunately, all these mechanisms are for a certain group of people, and the rest suffers in their ignorance and misconduct.

Christianity and culture

Christianity provides the best moral principles that the world is fighting. When Christianity reached certain corners of the world it was viewed as terror religion. Some people took protection of Christianity to propagate their own agenda. And because of that, certain people hated Christianity to the highest level. They were told about the harms brought by Christianity based on racial prejudice. They would go to the extent of saying, Christianity is for the white people, and I always laugh, because the same people who refuse to accept Christianity viewing it as the white people's propagation are accepting certain material things from the same white people. It is just the plan of the devil to try to hinder the good things which Christianity can bring about to change the world. Christianity played a vital role in changing the state of people in many nations, and as days went by, the church implies to have lost its strength due to misconception and denigration planted by the devil in people's minds. Church leaders used to play a vital role in the communities, but today they are considered less educated and uniformed people.

Now how can a blind person lead others? How can a person in dark save the other in the same darkness? The community has become blinded due to its leaders who lead them with blindfolded eyes; hence even children are having a serious influence than the elderly within the same communities.

The world now needs radical people with the understanding of where the world is heading, who can take the radical decision to help those needs salvation. As long as Christians are watching this happening under their nose then the generation is doomed for destruction. It is for this reason that the lawlessness is gaining its momentum in the church.

Same sex marriages are given the room in the churches, and they are even buying themselves into positions of influence, to enable them dragging the church to courts in the event the church raises its voice again such an act. They have destroyed the general moral values in the community, now they want to bring the same lawlessness in the church, and the church is becoming too spiritual than the word itself not to see such things coming. May God help the church of Jesus Christ to see how the devil is busy planting a dangerous seed which will be difficult to uproot. Church is a living organism and life must be seen! If a church can accommodate

44

death in it that means it is no longer a church; thus, church leaders should keep life within it not to be blindfold like worldly leaders.

There are people doing some inappropriate things inside the church, and the church is giving them the room to do so. Churches have been made to be burgers by people who want to buy power and compromise the Christian values. Such people are not for the kingdom of God, rather are agents of the devil. They appear to be like angels of light, but once they get the influence they need, then they will start to show their true colors. Usually those are the people who have the guts to take the church to courts. They do not care about the damage they will cause, to them, their names must be justified. How can you call such people Christians? Those are the brood of vipers which John the Baptist once mention about in his sermon.

If the church can not be very careful, it will go back to the lukewarm position, where it can't understand and recognize the voice of God anymore. It is on this regard that I would like to advice church leaders to be very vigilant when putting people into leadership, because the devil is after power, and so are his agents. Therefore he has to do whatever it takes to help those people to get to the positions they constrain. To avoid such mistakes, the Holy Spirit must be consulted when putting people into positions. The spirit of discernment must be put to use in the church so that we be able to discern what is right at any given moment.

The church does not need the external help for it to be serviceable. Jesus is the head of the church, and he will take care of His church. No one should claim to have helped the church, if one bring such claim, which means he is not of the church, because no one can claim to have helped his/her house, yet it is your responsibility. Bringing money to church should not carry some conditions with it. Once it does, there is a spirit behind such financing. Some pastors have become seed sowing ground of the devil's plan. Acquisitiveness has become a source of church distraction. People have become lovers of money than the work of God. And because of these, the church has allowed misconducts to enter its doors. The bible says,

"If the foundation is destroyed, what can the righteous do?" (Psalm 11:3).

It is a time when church leaders must restore order and harmony in the body of Christ. Be spiritually led by the Holy Spirit and quit compromise when it comes to the work of God.

Church and worldly leaders

Christianity is a great foundation for the largest governing bodies in the world. But due to lack of discipline and unconsciousness of the potential in it, it has given power and authority to the unsaved. Unsaved leaders have taken the church to captivity under the influence of the dark world. To them what matters is the wealth and money that comes with it, not the dangers it carries.

It is a time when the Christian community should open its eyes and see the spirit behind these heads of states and the legislators. The church is the light of the world, but it has become contrary as the dark seems to overpower the light. How can one explain the scenario whereby the church is supposed to get instruction from a government on how to worship, who to allow to come and worship, who to allow to preach, and what time should worship be conducted? Moreover, how can one explain the changing of Laws on schools not to have scripture unions and not doing Lord's prayers at assemblies in a country so called Christian country and the church see it as normal? The church should be showing the light in all domains of life, and then the true morals values will be reserved. If not then, the same unlawful acts which we see in certain parts of the world will find its way into the entire world and ultimately the church will not breath, hence it will be crippled.

Baseline of Christian culture

The bible carries all the best morals the world may need to do well. There is absolutely nothing we can say the word of God lacks which is needed for the betterment of the world. Good governments, good health, good education, and success it's all part of the package which comes with the word of God. For the bible tells us that:

> "All scripture is given by inspiration of God, and is profitable for doctrine, for reproof, for correction, for instruction in righteousness, that the man of God may be complete, thoroughly equipped for every good work." (2Timothy 3:16, NKJV)

Consequently not making use of the word of God, it is just mere ignorance of what it is able to do, both in a person's life and to the community at large. The wisdom of God is far beyond any type of ruler-ship in the world. It is the ignorance of scriptures that makes Christians to miss the mark, and they will conclude that they are less influential. May the church arise and look back to the mind of God! That is why God urged the Israelites through Jeremiah to, "… ask for the old paths………, and walk in it." (Jer. 6:16). The way is set, let us ask how to go about it and what are the proper avenues to be followed?

The world does not have the new creation; it does not have new people either. It is the same old creation that is changing with generations, and with different discoveries. God has done His work once and for all, and He set His principles once for all. Everything we see today, it was done a long time before, what we so call new things, are just discoveries. So people should not be intimidated by these new discoveries, and then they think, our generation is better than the former, No! The same way God wanted people to fear Him in those days with their little discoveries; it is the same way God wants us to revere Him today.

There is no need for someone to give excuses of the time we are living as an instrument for loosing morals. We still have the same bible used then, and the same morals are still required of us in this generation. Therefore, let us look back and learn from those of old how they kept the fear of the Lord, and embrace those values, then we will find rest in our souls.

It is very true that the bible warns us of the time of lawlessness coming. According to Apostle Paul in his letter to Timothy, he made a special emphasis that he should stay away from the lawlessness that will creep into the world. He said:

"But know this, that in the last days perilous times will come: For men will be lovers of themselves, lovers of money, boasters, proud, blasphemers, unloving, unforgiving, slanderers, without self-control, brutal, despisers of good, traitors, headstrong, haughty, lovers of pleasure rather than lovers of God, having a form of godliness but denying its power. And from such people turn away!" (2Timothy 3: 1-5, NKJV)

These things were foreseen, and indeed we are living in that time, but does that mean we should fold our hands and do nothing, No! Paul tells Timothy to stay away.

Now, as the church it is our responsibility to teach the people whom the Lord calls into His kingdom; so that they stay away from these acts and be on the safe side. The generation we are living in, people no longer care about their live anymore. As long one can have enough in their pockets, and be able to spoil themselves, it is good enough for them. So to them whatever means that brings money is always welcome, it does not matter in which way did it came, what they want it is their needs met. Because of these, they don't mind loosing their dignity and get what they want.

The church should then be on the steering wheel and help the communities to regain its morals. This can begin with community programs, like counseling, social works, and many other helping activities. It has to venture into its soul winning position through missionary works and evangelism programs. The main idea is to find ways of reaching out to the people on the ground level, for them not to get corrupt in the long run. Church should come up with means of the child developing programs, and this will help to train children at an early stage, and by the time they grow up, they would have learnt the good things which they must follow as they grow.

As previously alluded in the beginning passages of this chapter that, children needs much attention before the age of five for them to do the right thing. Once we miss that, it becomes difficult at a later stage to turn them to the right direction. Parents, Teachers and ministers at churches can play a vital role to change the community and the world at large in as far as culture is concerned.

CHAPTER SEVEN

Understanding the Time

"See then that you walk circumspectly, not as fools but as wise, redeeming the time, because the days are evil." (Ephesians 5:15-16, NKJV)

Many generations have lost directions, opportunities, and vision due to a lack of understanding of time. Time is an important commodity that needs to be understood. Failure to understand time leads to destruction of one's future and destine. Time has been there from the beginning and everything was conveniently done. There is no future or past without time, all is compacted within it. Every individual, nation, tribe, generation, activities, and circumstances are well identified by time. It is in this commodity that people well measure their success.

When God created the world, He made sure that everything was given its time of creation. In all His creation He could count His success and would say, "It is good." Making sure that things are done to the standard serves time as it minimizes repetition. He worked for six days, which we are not sure, how long the day was for the sun and moon which helps us to count the day and night now, was not there before time. In other words, time was made by God, not by His creation. He is the master of time because He started it.

All is well timed

Within six days, He created everything, and we are told that on the sixth day He rested. It is for this reason that a man of wisdom, King Solomon tells us that:

"To everything there is a season, a time for every purpose under heaven: A time to be born, and a time to die; A time to plant and a time to pluck what is planted; A time to kill, and a time to heal; A time to break, and a time to build-up; A time to weep, and a time to laugh; A time to mourn, and a time to dance; A time to cast away stones, and a time to gather stones; A time to embrace, and a time to refrain from embracing; A time to gain, and a time to lose; A

time to keep, and a time to throw away; A time to tear, and a time to sew; A time to keep silence, and a time to speak; A time to love, and a time to hate; A time to war, and a time of peace." (Ecclesiastes 3:1-8, NKJV).

Virtually all the activities happening in the world are summed up in this passage of the scriptures. This then means, God saw all these happening, and He made a provision for all of them in order for the humanity to understand time. No one in the world, who is born out of a woman, can say I never went through any of these. And the reality is, if one did not go through any of these, then, without fail, more is yet to come. Some escapes certain things, presumably, but there is one which none can not escape, which is the time of birth and time of death. If God had to rest from the work He did in six days, who are we not to take a rest from a certain number of years we live in this world.

Now, the biggest issue here is not about death itself, rather it is about how we are going to finish the race. Are we going to say like God, "it is good"? Will our work be counted as good even in our own sight? Can we honestly say, I must go and rest, for I have finished my course? Will the phrase "rest in peace," apply in our lives? If all or any of these questions are not, 'yes,' then you need to do a postmortem of your life and see what needs to be done.

Life span of our time

In the days we are living, the majority is dying at the age between 35 and 50 years for different reasons. A small fraction lives up to 70, and a countable goes beyond 80 years. Therefore, if the days of living are this much limited, will we be able to carry out our mandate and be satisfied of our work here on earth? For the thirty-five years I have lived, it feels like I have come far, but in reality, I can see that, I have not done much yet. You might be someone like me, having the same feeling, but the question is, what are you doing with your time?

We are living in a generation that has lost touch with time. A generation that does not care of the life they are heading. As long as they have what they want today, tomorrow is never in their calendar. The past is not known, and they do not bother to look back and check if there is anything to learn or correct and find the solution for their future life. Young people have lost the sense of progress, and there is no more hope in them. They live to dissipate their parents' bequest and never think about how their own children will subsist. The reason the world riches are going to a small group of people, I believe, it is because our generation has become negligent.

No one needs to take advice anymore and the parents' instructions have become a laughing matter to them. They leave home giving parents false hope that the kids are going to school, and meters away from home, they are into drugs. May the Lord come to the rescue of this generation and bring peace to the parents! My heart bleeds when I see schoolchildren smoking marijuana, on their way to school, and publicly; then in the afternoon you see the same child, at the robot begging for a lift to go back home. To them, going to school is just to meet with friends and give a false hope to the parents. In all these, authorities turn a blind eye, and to most parents, the plight has gone out of hand. The future of those young people is destroyed, and it takes God's grace for them to get it back. They cannot catch up with time and it has gone out of their hand. That means this is a generation that has lost its future, and to rebuild such, it is a mountain to climb.

Watch out of this time

It is on this note that the Apostle Paul addressing the church of Ephesus, he reminds them to, "*Walk circumspectly, not as fools but as wise,*" (Eph. 5: 15); the reason being, "*The days are evil.*" We are living in an evil generation, whereby anything that we do if we are not wise, we may find ourselves in a ditch. Once we are in that ditch, it becomes difficult to get out of it. Many people started little by little to make quick monies, by stealing, robbing, and doing all sorts of unlawful activities. After a diminutive while, they realize that, there was no revolving back, and their lives are doomed.

One day I met a certain a man, and he told me that, what he did was very terrible such that he could not turn back from it, He was roped in it and he was saying he might die in it. He was a robber, wanted by police everywhere, and he was breathing in that dynamism, he was afraid even to communicate with his own parents fearing that even they could report him to the police. But how did that started, little by little!

It is better to spend that little time doing something good, for in due season you can get good results out of it. **Time well spend is time well invested**! Successful people are the people who have managed well their time. I am not only talking about the success in the material things, but I would like us to consider our spiritual lives. Every minute we spend doing something contrary to God's will, it is a moment we will forever regret. God did not put us on earth to just live and die; he gave each and everyone of us a purpose of living.

Fulfilling the Purpose of life

The most painful thing is for a person to die without accomplishing his goal. Moses in his prayer he said:

"So teach us to number our days that we may gain a heart of wisdom." (Psalm 91:12).

How can one be able to number the days of their lives? Counting years is one of the easiest things I saw especially in this generation. People know their birthday more than they know the number of clothes they wear. From sleep you can ask someone their years they can yawningly tell you the exact day they were born. But that does not advance anyone because even the animal's days can be counted.

To number the days of living, one needs to count the successes he made in life. If you can look back and see what you have successfully done, then you can learn from such, and improve it to better your future. The more successful you accomplish your purpose that is the easier it become to number the days of your life.

God did not spend time idling for six days! We can count what He did in those six days before He took a rest. Let me correct a certain misconception in other people's minds. Rest is not for lazy people; Rest is for those who are committing themselves to work and accomplishes their purpose. If a person did not work why would he need to rest? God is expecting everyone to work and finish his or her race. Apostle Paul says:

"I have fought the good fight, I have finished the race, I have kept the faith. Finally, there is laid up for me the crown of righteousness, which the Lord, the righteous Judge, will give to me on that Day, and not to me only but also to all who have loved His appearing." (2Timothy 4:7-8, NKJV)

Paul knew his mandate, and he was entirely sure that his work was finished. He perfectly calculated his time and knew that he was ready to leave.

Chaotic life

Most people because of chaotic life they are living, it becomes difficult for them to know what time it is. They do not know what to do, and what needs to be done. Jim Muncy in his book **Time Basics** said this:

"If the world we lived in was a naturally ordered place, time management would be easy. But it is not. I look at pictures out into the universe from most advanced telescopes and I am amazed at the order. I talk to a biochemist and he explains in incredible detail the order that occurs at the smallest cluster of atoms, everything seem to have this intricate order and structure to it. That is, everything except my daily life." (**Basic Times, 2014, p.65**)

Some other people are just living, living a life without direction. They are taken by any wind that comes their way. Their spiritual life is not organized, neither is their general life organized. They only live today, and tomorrow it is a daydream. It is because of this reason that people can turn to anything that makes them survive. Corruption has increased due to this behavior. Drug abuse has increased due to the same behavior. Young people are carried away by disastrous activities due to a lack of understanding of the time they are living. The devil is taking most of the people's time with unproductive activities.

We are now living in a digital world, and technology has increased. This is not only affecting the young people, but even the elderly people are trap into our time's danger. Married people did not only waste time, but some have lost their marriage due to this change of time. Can we say the technology is bad? No! It is very good, and it came to save us from being busy bodies, trying to run around fixing issues. But unfortunately people due to ignorance of the time we are living in, they misused the good opportunity, and have become slaves to it; hence they have lost their time management.

We are in the end times

Considering the signs we are seeing, and how prophesies of the bible are matching the current activities, we can see that we are living in the last days. In these days we are living, it then needs people with a better understanding on how to lead their lives. It requires wisdom from above for us to calculate the time we are living. Moreover, that wisdom we can get it from the word of God. The world sees everything as normal, and it is we who are enlightened who should read and understand. It is not normal the way that children are rebelling against their parents; it is not normal the way in which marriages are breaking; it is not normal how nations are rising against each other; it is not even normal how the number of false prophets is increasing; neither is it normal how the lawlessness is increasing.

The church now needs the people like the sons of Issachar who understood the times, and they knew what Israel was ought to do. (1 Chronicles 12:32). Christians needs to be vigilant and hold on to their faith. Jesus gave a parable to His disciple in the book of Luke and at the end of the parable He asked this question; *"Nevertheless, when the Son of Man comes, will He really find faith on the earth?"* (Luke 18:8).

55

Every Christian should think about these words and hold on to what we have believed. Things around us should not change us; instead, we must influence the surroundings by what we believe. The world is in dark, what they see is the crisis and troubles brewing. They are busy fighting against the wind, whilst the real object stands. The real enemy of our time is the same old enemy the devil who is working so hard to draw back many people from their faith and win them over to his kingdom.

Time of visitation

In the book of Genesis, we are given a story of the Noah generation. Those people did not understand the time of their visitation. Noah was given a message for them to build an ark, but they could not comprehend the whole conception. They were living their lives to the fullness, and someone comes and tells them that God will destroy them; it was sarcastic to them. But the person who understood time built the ark and saved his family.

We see again in the book of Jonah that the people of Nineveh were gentiles; they knew nothing much about the God of heaven. When God wanted to destroy their nation, Jonah was sent to preach to them. Regardless of their stubbornness, by hearing the preaching of Jonah, they repented and fasted for some days for God to serve them. Yet God could not destroy them, for He had mercy on them. The reason of their salvation it was their understanding of God's time of visitation.

The children of Israel on the other hand did not understand the time of their visitation. Luke reports Jesus' message to the unbelieving Jews saying:

"If you had known, even you, especially in this your day, the things that make for your peace! But now they are hidden from your eyes. For days will come upon you when your enemies will build an embankment around you, surround you and close you in on every side, and level you, and your children within you, to the ground; and they will not leave in you one stone upon another, because you did not know the time of your visitation." (Luke 19: 42-44, NKJV)

However, we cannot be like them, for the knowledge is given to us, therefore we have to know what needs to be done. We are the children of light, and we should be able to detect anything that may pull us from God's presence. May the Lord give us an understanding of the time we are living!

Corrupt generation

Peter addressing his listeners on the day of Pentecost he pleaded with them saying, *"Save yourselves from this corrupt generation."* (Acts 2:41, NIV). The same message should ring in our ears as in the days of the early church, we need to save ourselves. The time we are living is very corrupt; all that we see are the minority succeeding and majority suffering. In the back of other people's mind, they think it is hard work paying, No. People are corrupt and they are doing whatever they can only for the love of money. Anything that makes them to find a living it is a blessing to them, the source do not matter to them.

Not everything is meant for us, for darkness cannot mix with light. We cannot associate ourselves with evil dealings, for it will spoil the good works of God in us. We are of God, and He is our source of provision in all that we need.

Therefore, we do not have to walk as fools, we need to know our enemy, we need to defend our faith and stand our ground. We are given all the tools we need to both know and use in any given time. The word of God is there to guide us in the proper way, and the Holy Spirit will show us the proper direction. We don't have to miss the mark due to our ignorance, lets yield to the Spirit of the Lord, let Him help us to understand the times. He is able to help us to detect all the danger zones so that we do not fall in the trap of the devil.

CHAPTER EIGHT

Miracles and Signs Seekers

"Then the Pharisees and Saducees came, and testing Him asked that He would show them a sign from heaven. He answered and said to them, 'When it is evening you say, it will be fair weather, for the sky is red; and in the morning, it will be foul weather today, for the sky is red and threatening. Hypocrites! You know the how to discern the face of the sky, but you cannot discern the signs of the times. A wicked and adulterous generation seeks after a sign, and no sign shall be given to it except the sign of Prophet Jonah.' And He left them and departed." (Matthew 16:1-4, NKJV)

The people of this generation have become a culprit of the foresaid 'wicked and adulterous generation,' a generation that seeks for signs, wonders and miracles, instead of seeking for salvation. What they need are the signs to prove to them that one is operating in power from heaven. If they cannot see miracles then to them the power of God does not exist within the church. Thus, because of this, many has become spiritual adulterous, and they have turned to other gods to try to gratify the desires of their flesh. They have turned to other gods to get powers to please the eyes of other people.

The hearts of many people have been hardened by the devil, such that, they cannot easily accept the gospel. To them, a sign must be seen and miracles must be evident before they can accept the credibility of the gospel. This has become a serious challenge to the wavering servants of God such that some without a firm foundation ended up going to seek for some powers from the dark world. They have gone excessively far from the presence of God and involve themselves in spiritual adultery and worshipped other gods for the sake of power and fame for people in their society.

Are signs and miracles bad? No! Signs, wonders and miracles are absolutely good, but once one begin to chase after them, then it becomes a serious trap, and the devil can take recognition of that, then he gives you what you are seeking after, but not for the good.

Operating in the power of God is essential, and it has to be in accordance with the scriptures. Trying to divert from the original way of performing signs and miracles in the scriptural way makes it bizarre and eventually scrutiny must be exercised to such actions. People want to see signs and wonders, yes! Nevertheless, the man of God should not be driven by people's pressure to work miracles; for we do not manufacture miracles, they do happen by the power of the Holy Spirit.

Self made signs and miracles

Other people have fallen into the hands of bogus ministers whom we call miracle makers. Technology has brought us some serious problems in this generation where people are busy looking for signs and miracles. Some people are now taking advantage of other people's ignorance and make them believe their tactical tricks which they so call signs and wonders. They play around with their minds and twist their focus with mere technological skills to make them believe what they see as true, yet nothing in reality will be a phenomenon.

It is very inopportune that even the leaders of nations and communities, most of them are still illiterate in as far as the technology is apprehensive, and they also plunge into the same ensnare. Once a minister, governor or and other person of a higher rank goes to such meetings where these things are happening, these miracle makers take advantage and runs to publish it to make people think that it is legit. They do all they can to push for their schema within a shot time, and by the time people's eyes are opened it will be too late.

How can someone explain that a person can dial a number from a cellphone and talk to God? How can someone even explain that a person can enter heaven with a Smartphone and take himself a selfie and then come back to show people the pictures of heaven? Have we become so foolish that people can play our minds to that extend? This is what happens when people are busy looking for signs and miracles; the devil will make you blind and bring to you some tactics to fulfill your expedition.

They have nothing in mind about the kingdom of God; neither are they to help make people to recognize the light through the word of God. What they want is people's money, and pleases their master, the devil. They will make sure that they milk people's money, and after that, they will disappear into the thick air and you will never hear of them again.

How can someone think of having a miracle like, from nowhere money just drops in the bank account and claim it as a miracle? One is told to bring an offering, and then miracle money will appear in their account, like seriously? Does God manufacture money in heaven and send His angels to put the money in one's account over night? Can God change the writings of the bank overnight and make your account to have a record of more money without any trace?

People who teach and encourage people in such wrongdoing have to be punished by the law because none of the bible verses suggests such. However, unfortunately, because our justice systems and the authorities are too corrupt such that they take part in milking their citizens. They are made to believe that such things are biblical and it is within our religion to do such. No! The devil blinded their eyes so that they may not see.

They sale natural things like water, cooking oil, stones and so on in the name of the bible. They are not charged any tax, in the name of the bible. They make citizens poor in the name of the bible. In nations where people claim to be, wise and educated, but cannot intervene to help their citizens who abused by people who hide behind the bible. Anyway, do they have any solutions? The answer to that is yes, but they are either corrupt or eye blinded. The only thing to do is to be silent and watch people suffer more as they dive into the pool of poverty.

The devil is using these people to make other people poor and bring all the riches in the hands of a few so that his mission can be accomplished. When people have become poor, they will then start to beg for help and he (devil) will bring them into his kingdom and make them suffer more. All this is an outcome of seeking for signs and miracles. The devil takes advantage of what people are longing for, and he brings into their eyes a counterfeit solution and makes them believe it as real. May the Lord help us to see what is right and make the right decisions of our lives? May He enable us to pinpoint the true and self-made signs and miracles?

Dark world signs and miracles

Since people of this age are in a drive to search and look for signs and miracles. The devil is also at work advancing his methods of miracles and signs to beguile them. For many generations we have known of magic and counterfeit miracles. The bible gives us many examples of how the dark world could counterfeit miracles and signs. The purpose was only to make people believe the contrary, leaving the reality of God's wonderful works.

The generation we are living in has not departed from such activities, and the devil is pleased to find people who are partaking in fulfilling his purpose. Some people have gone to the extent of selling their souls to the devil for them to gain fame and power. Some are even coming out of the church and went to look for those powers and entice the people of God in a way of diverting them from the truth of God. They get powers to implement signs; they will get powers to work false healing even do the improbable things.

It is very important for us to know that witches can plant a sickness in the life of a person and they have means of removing it. Their purpose in doing that, it will be for self- glory, and win people over into their occult in essence to the devil. Hence, if someone is not careful, he may be convinced that they have the power, yet they are reversing their deeds or sickness out of you.

Most of the miracles people are now experiencing in so many places in the name of the church are becoming questionable. How can someone get pregnant and within some days, not months, not even weeks, and give birth? After giving birth the

61

child cannot even last, then we call that a miracle? Can God do a half miracle? How can He allow a child to be born as a miracle baby, then instead of making the child to bring glory to His name, then the child dies?

The world needs to open its eyes and see how the devil is playing with their minds and eyes. The power of darkness is at work, and many people have given their lives to accomplish that purpose. We do not have to believe every miracle; rather we should discern the spirit behind the healing. To start with, we have to look at the conduct of the minister and see if He is living according to God's word, and check the upbringing if he has traceable Christian life. Because Jesus warned us saying:

"Not everyone who says to Me, 'Lord, Lord,' Shall enter the kingdom of heaven, but he who does the will of My Father in heaven. Many will say to Me in that day, 'Lord, Lord, have we not prophesied in Your name, cast out demons in Your name, and done many wonders in Your name?' And then I will declare to them, 'I never knew you; depart from Me, you who practice lawlessness!'" (Matthew 7:21-23)

Therefore, let us not believe every miracle, sign or wonder, but let's be critical and seek to know if it is from God and if God is really working with that minister. By failure to do so, we should be careful that we may fall into the hands of the enemy, and follow him forever into destruction. The Bible recommends us to test the spirits so that we do not fall into the trap of the wicked.

Biblical miracles

The bible is the book of miracles, signs and wonders. What we see being portrayed in the bible are miracles and wonders throughout. Therefore, signs, miracles and wonders are real, and they do happen. We have seen, so many people healed in the bible times, so many wonders happening, and God has shown so many signs. This then means miracles, signs and wonders do happen, and God uses His people to works those wonders.

True signs and miracles are produced by the power of the Holy Spirit. The LORD told Zerubbabel through Zachariah that:

"Not by might nor by power, but by My Spirit,' Says the LORD of hosts." (Zach. 4:6).

All the supernatural activities are just by the work of the Holy Spirit. If the Holy Spirit is not involved in any wonder, then one should know that the power of darkness is at work. Every person who claim to do signs and miracles and denies the power of the Holy Spirit, we have to disqualify that person from being a legitimate Christian miracle minister.

Jesus Christ is our perfect example of how miracles should be done. The primary purpose of Bible miracles, signs and wonders were for the glory of God. Every miracle Jesus Christ our Lord performed was for the glory of God. He did not do miracles to please His viewers. And the bible gives us a report of His respond when people got a wrong perception of His way of performing miracles. And it says:

"Then those men, when they had seen the sign that Jesus did, said, 'This is truly the Prophet who is to come into the world.' Therefore when Jesus perceived that they were about to come and take Him by force to make Him king, He departed again to the mountain by Himself alone." (John 6:14-15, NKJV)

So here, we see a people that were looking for signs and wonders, and when they found what they wanted, the next thing they wanted him to become their leader (king). But Him knowing His purpose and whom He was doing it for, He ran away from self glory. This should be the attitude of every the man of God, whom God is using for His glory; and anyone who takes glory to himself is not a man of God and He is a worker of another kingdom, not of God.

Sickness is never permanent. Every sick person is meant to be healed or will die with that sickness. In either way, sickness is not permanent, but it is for one to learn to fear God. Therefore, when God is healing a person, it is only for His glory, and that person should give God praise, not any of God's creation.

What destroys many people is pride; they perform a miracle today, they start to walk chest out saying, 'I have done it.' This is how the cult of personality begins. The next thing this person wants to be called by names for self-glory. Moreover, pride will breathe to the fullness and eventually he falls.

A true minister of God according to the word of God, works miracles with God, and knows how to give God credit. **A miracle is not meant to live forever, but it is given for a certain purpose.** God has created all things perfectly, but certain conditions are like that, for God's glory (John 9: 1-3). So when a miracle, sign or wonder happen, it does not surprise God for He knows why is it like that. It is only us the human beings who can be surprised; for it looks new in our sight. It is God who works a miracle, sign or wonder, at His given time and circumstances. He is not moved by a man to do so, but by His own will.

Therefore, seeking for miracles, signs and wonders it is a sign that one does not know God, and is still far from understanding the kingdom principles. A miracle does not take a person to heaven; neither does it make a person a Christian. **A miracle does not show a person the gate to heaven, but gives people the eyes to see the works of God.** A sign, wonder or miracle, can make or break people, if they didn't understand God's principles.

God is never far from anyone of us, He is near every creature. One needs not to seek for a miracle, but the kingdom of God. It is in the kingdom of God that we find our help. Peace, joy and happiness are found in the kingdom of God. We are going to see in the last chapter that; all we need is found in Jesus Christ, and once we found Him, miracles are not a thing to be sort after.

We do not need to create a room for the devil to find glory in the way we behave. Now is the time when we should seek to know how God wants us to live, and by so doing our lives will be full of signs and wonders, and we will live joyously. Let us not fall into the trap of the devil by following teachings that leads us into the hands of the enemy (the devil); where he will use us as he wishes, then afterwards destroy us.

CHAPTER NINE

Music and Entertainments

"For the wrath of God is revealed from heaven against all ungodliness and unrighteousness of men, who suppresses the truth in unrighteousness, because what may be known of God is manifest in them, for God has shown it to them." (Romans 1:18-20, NKJV)

Suppression of the truth in unrighteousness is visibly seen in music and entertainment industries. Most of the young people are getting out of control due to music and entertainment. They start little by little until they are uncontrollably addicted to it. People are loosing direction and being lost from the proper direction by what they are watching and listening to on a daily basis.

Music was meant for a good purpose, but the devil has found a tool of distraction within it, hence he is sharpening it for his personal gain. People no longer listen to music for edification, but rather for fleshly gratification. Singing has been meant to be for the glory of God, but it has been diverted to bring affections in the hearts of people. As time went by through to our generation, the evil world has found it perfect to use music even to drag many people into the kingdom of darkness.

Entertainment on the other hand has grown rapidly in different forms. In the past age band, people had their way of entertainment, which was properly guided by their cultural conducts. But in our generation, entertainment took another dimension with the increase of technology in this digital world.

Televisions are providing certain entertainment, which to some point is partially controlled by state; whilst on the other hand internet has brought a serious trouble to today's people. Many things from the dark world have taken its habitation in the world of internet.

Musical influence

In most domains of the world, people are seeking for powers. And they believe that they can not perform to the best without such powers, hence they have sold themselves into the hands of the enemy, the devil.

So many musicians are operating under the power of darkness. And music has become the most dangerous tool the devil is using to destroy most of our youngsters. Innocent kids are being initiated into the dark world through some music they are listening. They are being lured by certain music and ignorantly they will find themselves involved in certain satanic dealings. People's ears are now itching to listen to things, and whatever that pleases their ears its superior for them. For as long what they hear is making their heart to be at easy, they do not mind its source. Some do not evening mind about who wrote it and worse still, they careless of the meaning of the lyrics in the song. Gradually and surely, their spirit is stolen through emotions and they found themselves ensnared in the kingdom of darkness unintentionally.

Youngsters are the most vulnerable these days in as far as music is concerned. They follow whatever that is trending, and inconsiderately they become lost and get carried away such that they become uncontainable. Parents are not doing enough to teach their children in these mere things. They let their children to listen to any music which they don't even understand themselves and conclude that it is today's music. What manner parent are they; who allows the children in their domicile to get information they do not understand and give credit to the increase of technology and the era we are living?

Every parent has the right to know what their children are listening to and educate them in the right music to listen. Parents do not need to be irresponsible and blame it on illiterate. If one needs to remain in control of their family in this age bracket, he needs to acquaint himself with the current systems at any cost. Time is changing, and those who are grown up must not be lazy and remain in their cocoon of their old epoch.

Churches and its leaders are the other helping hand who should help in educating its people on the type of music to play, not to allow every kind of music that comes their way without proper inspection. Nevertheless, it is unfortunately that some other churches just adopt any form of music without scrutinizing the source, as long the song sounds good it is a done deal.

Music can destroy people silently, but effectively. The devil is entering churches through music, and his agents are being planted in churches through musicians and singers. I have known of many musicians in churches who are not born again, and they are given chances to serve because of their understanding of music. Do the leaders know where they learnt their music? Do the leaders have a traceable record of their Christian lives? And did we know their well-about spiritually? If the church can not do a checklist of all these, then chances are high that they may allow their music to be infiltrated by the devil.

Music is supposed to be a blessing, and it has to bring glory to our living God. And every source of music must be thoroughly scrutinized and see if it really glorifies God. There is a certain kind of music which does not really contain God in them, but the fact that it is mentioning something first-class in it; we conclude that, 'it is good.'

Before we conclude and qualify it, let's get to know the author, and try to understand the mind of the author, to see if he/she meant it for God, or something else. This will help us not to promote the work of the dark world in the church by mere mistake of not considering the purpose of that music. It is on this regard, I pray to God that He raises many musicians within our own churches, to sing for us the songs we understand and bring glory to God.

Let us save each other by helping to have understanding when it comes to music. Church leaders and all parents should acquaint themselves with what is happening in today's world in order for them to be relevant and guard against profligacy. This will help to preserve our youngsters and also keep aliveness of the future generations.

Entertainment influence

The level at which entertainments is growing and increasing has reached an alarming level. The age group that is to come is likely to suffer some serious consequences. We are living in a generation that has too much ideas of doing things and technology has brought lots of creativeness in people. Many people are now devising ways of making people get entertained, and in so doing, there is much confusion on what is right and what is wrong.

The number of television channels has increased, and each one of them comes with many entertainments for both elderly and young people. All entertainers have goals to settle, and they can do all they can to win the hearts of their viewer. In trying to win the hearts of people, some have gone far, into other worlds seeking for powers to attract viewers. And it is very sad to note that once they perform, many people may not realize the spirit behind their actions up to a later stage.

People perform in a certain way and dressing in certain ways, we see nothing wrong in it, but little did we know that we are being transformed with such proceedings. Nowadays we see some youngsters acting somehow, talking somehow, and dressing somehow. Have we ever asked ourselves how did it come about?

This generation is completely lost, and parents are doing nothing to bring harmony in their families. They easily hoodwinked by their children to accept and believe that it is the era we are living. Leaders and parents are no longer in charge of how their people or children should behave, or wear, but it is in the power of certain individuals whom we are not sure of their origin. They are remote controlling our youngsters in our sight and with our permission.

Kids like their cartoons, and they understand things better through cartoons. But it is pathetic that the evil doers are now trying to introduce child porno through these cartoons. They make some cartoons showing love affairs, a male figure kissing a female figure. What do you think a child of 5 years does when they see such kind of events? Of course the next thing is, they want to experiment what they saw happening. You will find out that a girl of 7 years wants to have an affair or want an elderly person to kiss her. Where did she found that from? The television!

Levels of rape cases are increasing, and some of these are emanating from what youngsters are seeing happening and eventually they want to experience such things. And in their quest to do that, sometimes they behave somehow to an adult person, and if the adult person lacks discipline, then rape is committed.

Again with the increase of digital devices, people are now doing weird things behind curtains. You will see a person quiet but busy with their phones on a corner, a careful consideration should be done there. Internet is now filled with too much junk, and the main idea of that junk is to twist the minds of people. Children are the most vulnerable to that. The devil has shifted his focus to the new generation, for he knows that the elderly people are passing, so if he can capture the young ones, then he will control the future generations as he wills. Pornography of all kinds has been planted on worldwide websites. Whatever people want to know about sex, they can just Google search and get what they want.

Our children are now demanding to have phones, not for them to use for researches as they may say, but to search for weird things. The problem is, once they search and find what they want, then the next things they want to experiment, and eventually, they are lost.

At school children no longer concentrate in their studies, they are always busy chatting and sending each other nude pictures and videos when parents are busy working for them to better their future. They no longer regard their lecturers, for they think they have it all. They have reduced their teachers to their level, for they think, they can not teach them any longer. At the end when they fail, their parents will be on the neck of the teachers accusing them of not doing enough to make their children to pass. And what do you expect teachers to do?

I heard of other places now where teachers are even being pressured to add marks for the kids so that the parents won't go mad with them for the failure of their children. These people are innocent; it is us the parents who are making their job to be complicated. We are destroying our generation, and the future of our children is at jeopardy here.

The number of marriages breaking is increasing. And one of the reasons for breakages, it is blamed on how people are handling entertainment especially on social media. Some people ignorantly, they are no longer able to handle their partners. Their partners are busy watching certain friction that is happening on televisions, and after, they would like the same to be done in the house, and when the other partner fails, then they want to look for someone who can do it better. So have our cultures, religious teachings and all the ways we were taught being reduced to nothing with mere entertainment of these days?

Who then, shall deliver this generation from this entire catastrophe? Is there any hope of the future generations? Will the future generation be able to straighten all these meandering? Actually, is it everything that we will be able to change even if the chance will be given?

Honestly not everything can be restored, but the solution of these is evident and it is for the people whose hearts are to be saved. And in the next chapter we will try to bring a solution to all these problems that have engulfed the world in our time.

CHAPTER TEN

Jesus Christ is the Only Answer

"For God so loved the world that He gave His only begotten Son, that whoever believes in Him should not perish but have everlasting life; For God did not send His Son into the world to condemn the world, but that the world through Him might be saved." (John 3:16-17, NKJV)

The world has reached the crossroads, and people are thrown into bewilderment, and they do not know what to believe. So many things are happening, and some are loosing their faith, due to the positions they find themselves. People's hope has been weakened, and everything they see in future is just darkness. Looking at the current situations, in their families, profession, studies, businesses, and worse still their spiritual life; all they see is hopeless.

Is there any hope again in this age bracket? How about the generation to come, are they going to make it? Will we see again the glorious times when people could count on the future of their age group? If so, who can bring such a kind of hope? These are the questions people are asking in their hearts, and they wish to know what comes next.

The authorities seem to be clueless of how they will handle the future of their cohort. Spiritual leaders are supposed to mend the way through spiritual guidance, but it suggests they too are in uncertainty. All that the leaders are seeing with the current trade in the world is just a hopeless future.

It is for this reason that people needs to be pointed to the original plan of God on humanity. If we can't see the way properly, the best way is to ask the one who walked on it; and get knowledge from the architecture of humanity.

God is the master of time and circumstances, and He knows what this age band is facing. He absolutely knew about it some ages ago, and He then has an unadulterated plan for all the generations to come. He provided a solution for the challenges long before the creation of the world. So He is not caught by a bolt from the blue of the current episode. The rebellion of people, disrespectfulness of people, challenges of the change of times; all these He foresaw it from the beginning of times.

So what we are seeing as new now, in God's calendar it has already happened. Therefore He has put a plan of action before all these things started happening. It all began in the Garden of Eden when men sinned against God as we have already alluded in the preceding chapters. There and then, God promised a solution to the current situation, and He said:

"And I will put enmity between you and the woman, and between your seed and her Seed; He shall bruise your head, and you shall bruise His heel." (Genesis 3:15, NKJV)

God promised a Seed that would come and crush the head of the enemy. And that Seed, it is Jesus Christ. It is in that Seed that the world still finds hope, and He guarantees the future of our age group, and the generations to come.

The hope of our Salvation

We have only one hope in the life we are living. We people in all nations (even though some are adamant), our hope is in Jesus Christ. The Apostle Paul in his message to the Galatians said:

"Now I say that the heir, as long as he is a child, does not differ at all from a slave, though he is master of all, but is under guardians and stewards until the time appointed by the father. Even so we, when we were children, were in bondage under the elements of the world. But when the fullness of the time had come, God send forth His Son, born of a woman, born under the law, to redeem those who were under the law, that we might receive the adoption as sons." (Galatians 4:4-5, NKJV)

Our redemption was promptly set by God, and He knew the exact time the world would need the redeemer. He sent for us the promised Seed to come and deliver us from the power of darkness. He did not come for a particular people, but for the whole world. John report and say:

> *"He came to His own, and His own did not receive Him. But as many as received Him, to them He gave the right to become children of God, to those who believe in His name: who were born, not of blood, nor of the will of the flesh, nor of the will of man, but of God."* (John 1:11-13, NKJV)

So the privilege has been given to everyone, and this point to any human being living on this earth. It is our own choice to decide to receive Him or not. He does not impose Himself on people; rather He gives them scope to choose. But the most important thing is that, He is the one who can give us hope, for it is Him who has the power to crush the head of the enemy, and bring freedom in our lives.

The hope of our generation and its future is found in Jesus; for He will never fail us. He gives us hope, in today's world, and in the future era. Which means, even if we face the challenges of this globe, we can still live a peaceful life in Christ perpetually. When He comes into our lives, He gives us a peaceful mind, and we will not be tossed to and fro, by every wind that blows in this world. We will find rest in Him.

Co-yoke bearer

The yokes people are bearing have become too heavy to the point that they cannot bear them any longer. From all sides, people have lost peace, and they always wish to die than to live with the challenges of life. The level of suicide has increased due to troubles of this age. Number of divorces has increased due to mistrust, and dishonest. Rebellious children have caused the early death of their parents; hence the number of orphanage has increased. Indeed it is too much to bear it! But we have a man who is willing to help us carry the burden.

Jesus Christ is inviting anyone with any kind of burden to come to Him. A yoke is not meant to be carried by one man, but rather two who walks side by side. Jesus is offering a hand to your problem, and He wants to exchange His yoke with yours. For He says;

> *"Come to Me, all you who labor and are heavy laden, and I will give you rest. Take My yoke upon you and learn from Me, for I am gentle and lowly in heart, and you will find rest for your souls. For My yoke is easy and My burden is light."* (Matthew 11:28-30, NKJV)

He is inviting us to take a walk with Him, in a hard-hitting and unbearable situation. This means He will walk side by side with us. Neil T. Anderson gives us an insight of this verse, and he said; "Being yoked with Jesus does not mean we sit around thinking pious thoughts expecting God to do it all. Nor does it mean running around in endless activities trying to do it all by ourselves. It is a walk with the only One who knows the way, who is the truth, and has the life to make it possible. In Him we find rest for our souls, for His yoke is easy and His burden is light." In addition, He went on saying, "With all the harshness and vulgarity surrounding us in this fallen world, we have been invited to walk with the gentle Jesus. Imagine that!" (**Renewing your mind, 2014, p.46**)

Therefore there is no need for us to suffer on our corner; we have a helper who is present in times of need. He is inviting everyone today to come unto Him. He loves us, and He can not allow us to head for destruction. We can come to Him with any trouble which has become a thorn in our flesh and He can set us free.

In any plight, Jesus is our co-yoke bearer; He carries the burden with us. He hears us when we call on His name for help, and He can speedily reach us for help. He will walk us through all the troubles of this present generation, till the world to come where we will live with Him forever.

The Way, the Truth, and the Life

"Jesus said to him, 'I am the way, the truth, and the life. No one comes to the Father except through Me.'" (John 14:6, NKJV)

(a) The Way

Jesus Christ is not only the burden bearer, but He is the Way. He helps us to carry the burden, and guide us through, for He is the Way. He does not lead us through the path He has never travelled; but He guides us through the way Himself created. Many people wonder, what will happen in the future, and they found themselves in a panic mood. I want to assure us that it is not necessary, for there is one who knows all the future ahead of us. One who travelled all the way before us, He will prepare a best way for our future generations.

The way may sound to be tough, and there may be a collection of huddles in it, but we are certain that our Lord will never leave us nor forsake us. David has experienced the importance of following the way giver, and he says:

"The LORD is my shepherd; I shall not want. He makes me to lie down in green pastures; He leads me beside still waters. He restores my soul; He leads me in the paths of righteousness for His name's sake. Yeah, though I walk through the valley of the shadow of death, I will fear no evil; For You are with me; Your rod and Your staff, they comfort me. You prepare a table before me in the presence of my enemies; You anoint my head with oil; My cup runs over. Surely goodness and mercy shall follow me all the days of my life; and I will dwell in the house of the LORD forever." (Psalm 23, NKJV)

Therefore, it is very important to have this kind of understanding, that as long as the Lord is with us, we will be on the safe side. Jesus is the only Way, He will not only guide us in this life, but He provides a way for us to the Father.

(b) The truth:

He is also the truth the world is trying to search for. Reasons why people are moving from one place to another trying to find a solution to different things, it is because they are never satisfied with what they know. For ages now, people has been trying to discover God in different methods, to the extent that some are now worshiping idols; whilst others have concluded that a mere man from their tribe is the solution to their problems. The only truth we found satisfying is Jesus Christ. Elmer Towns said, "Christ was not only the way but also the truth in its absolute nature. He is the fountain and standard of truth." (**The Ultimate Guide to the Names of God, 2014, p.222**)

This then means whatever truth we may need, we can get it only in Christ Jesus. The world has been fooled by people who claim to be wise; and yet they came up with certain innovations, and made people to believe lies through their manipulation, and that has led people astray; hence we have too many religious movements these days. Apostle John records Jesus saying, *"And you shall know the truth, and the truth shall make you free."* (John 8:32).

This kind of truth is only found in the word of God. **Any truth that does not make a person free is not truth.** The truth should free a person, in any given environment. Many people are in different predicaments due to what they were told, and believed it to be true, yet in its essence it was a farce. May the Lord help us to embrace the real truth, which is Jesus Christ our Lord and Savior.

(c) The life

Jesus does not offer us a temporal life that only sustains us for some days in this age. I have seen many people in hospitals being sustained by machines to live longer, but eventually they die. When we talk about the life Jesus gives, we talk of eternal life, the life of God. Jesus is God, and when He gives us life, He gives us the Godly life, which is eternal. For He promised in the John 3 verse 16 that, "Whoever believes in Him should not perish but have everlasting life."

There is hope in Jesus Christ. Even if the condition in this current life is not favorable to us, but one thing we know is that whoever is in Christ, will rejoice again in the world to come. That hope is not for every person, but only for those who have believed in Jesus as the Son of the living God and accepted Him as the life giver.

Therefore by believing in Jesus, we find the Way in Him, the Truth, and Life. That is none negotiable, and there is no money to be paid, it is given freely. People waste lot of money looking for ways of life, finding the truth, and even trying to prolong their life. But I have good news for you today. We have found the true source of these three elements, His name is Jesus Christ. If you can hold on and cling to Him, you must be assured that your future is certain.

The Savior of the World

"He has delivered us from the power of darkness and conveyed us into the kingdom of the Son of His love, in whom we have redemption through His blood, the forgiveness of sins." (Colossians 1:13-14, NKJV)

The majority of the world has found themselves in positions they are not sure how they can come out of it. Some are in it for the love of money; others they were forced by certain challenges circumstances of life; whilst others inherited it from their families. Peace is a talk of the neighbors to them, and they do not know what a good sleep is. They have lost hope and they wish to die soon than to live long in such conditions of life. Some lost their friends and family, and all they have are their miserable lives. From outside it looks things are going well. When you see them walking, you may think they are the most favorable of this generation, but the reality is contrary.

Apostle Paul when addressing the people of Athens who did not know which God to worship and they turned to the gods they did not know; He said to them;

"Truly, these times of ignorance God overlooked, but now commands all men everywhere to repent, because He has appointed a day on which He will judge

the world in righteousness by the Man whom He has ordained. He has given assurance of this to all by raising Him from the dead." (Acts 17: 30-31, NKJV)

There is hope for every human being as long as we are still alive. One can make a choice today to quit any kind of dirty works they are doing and get saved. In whichever way one gets himself in any scene, the solution is found inside him, to choose whether to live in it or to come out of it. God has already provided a plan for their salvation, and He is ready to accept everyone with His two hands. What they need to do is to repent from their dead works and accept Jesus Christ as their Lord and saviour, and then they will be saved.

We were all in darkness one way or the other, but when we heard about Jesus, we made a choice to take Him into our lives. We no longer live in fear because our Hope lies in Him. He is the only savior who can set a person free. He had to die on the cross of Calvary for you and me, so that by believing in Him, we may live a peaceful life. The bible tells us that:

"But God demonstrates His own love towards us, in that while we were still sinners, Christ died for us." (Romans 5:8).

We are the cause of Christ's death. He did not deserve to die, for He was righteous, but due to the sin that was committed by our forefathers we needed someone to die for us.

Now our duty is only to believe in the one who died on our behalf then we will be set free. That is a free gift of God which He gave to us. He does not ask for anything from us, except to only believe in His Son, and then we will be saved. The choice still remain in us to choose what is good and evil. One can say I am content with living in my evil deeds and die in it. And another can decide to shun all the wrong doing and turn to Jesus Christ. Our salvation is in the obedience of the word of God. Like the writer of the book of Hebrew say, *"Today, if you will hear His voice, do not harden your hearts."* (Hebrews 4:7).

It is not too late for every human being to make a change, for as long as they live. The only place that does not have hope it's the memorial park; because, once life and body separates, then that person is completely lost if he is not saved.

What makes me to cry when someone has passed on it is not how they died, or the condition they left the family, but rather the condition of their spirit at the time of death. Because if one is born again, and they die, I am sure that one day, I will meet them; but the one who died without knowing Christ is forever lost. The bible tells us that: "For whoever calls on the name of the Lord shall be saved." (Romans 10:13).

By only calling on the name of the Lord, salvation is guaranteed. No matter how is the condition one might be facing, no matter the condition they found themselves; the name of Jesus is the only one that can deliver.

CHAPTER ELEVEN

Conclusion

In summary, the original plan of God towards the man was infiltrated and due to that, we are finding ourselves in this position. Sin has caused much harm, and its escalation has brought less hope in people about their future generations. People no longer have the idea of what to believe; and what they see is a darkened future because of the current prevailing circumstances.

People are not sure how to control the problem they orchestrated themselves. The very laws they made for themselves has become a snare, and it is now haunting them. They acknowledge its pressure in the household, community, everywhere and even in the governing bodies. No one is exempted of this beast called rebellious. It has started with small things and little by little it grew up with people's support, hence now the world has lost its direction.

Thank God for Jesus Christ. The world does not have any other hope except Jesus Christ. Jesus is the only hope we have, here on earth, and even in the future times. He is our only refuge, and if we decide to hide in Him, we will be safe. Psalms 91 verse1 tells us that: "He who dwells in the secret place of the Most High shall abide under the shadow of the Almighty."

We can choose to trust God for our safety, or deny Him for destruction. God's love is great such that He can not let us drawn in our troubles that is why He sent Jesus Christ to come and redeem us, out of the troubles our forefather Adam brought us.

Therefore, let us take this chance we are given at this moment and allow Him to give us the love we need. Our duty is to accept His love by acknowledging His Son Jesus Christ as the Lord and Savior, and then we will be saved. This will not only help us as individuals, but the future generations will as well find a hiding place and secure their live. God's arms are wide open to anyone who had taken their own direction who wants to come back to Him. Moreover, we have to remember that no mater the conditions we are in, His love will never fail us! In addition, He is the helper who is present to reach us in any challenge of life. May the good God bless us for taking a good decision to remap our lives!

BOOK NUGGETS

- To fear God, is to reverence Him, to do what He say, and live according to His precepts
- If people want to live successfully and have a life with full of days, the fear of the Lord is the key
- It is very important to guard our minds from the evil things of this world for man has fallen with their intelligence within the twinkling of an eye.
- The man was created a unique and awesome, and God did it knowing that the same creature, unique from any other creation, will glorify Him.
- The root cause of any sort of sin is disobedience.
- What pleases our eyes does not necessarily please God.
- I came to realize that, whatever said to us by the devil, whether good or evil, he remains the devil.
- It is not possible to straighten a crooked and bend sweet potato
- If someone wants to know who God is, he must get to know His Word.
- Children are a product of their quarters; they portray a true picture of how things are under the roof.
- The biblical leadership is of servant-hood, but today's leadership has become autocratic
- Any truth that does not make a person free is not truth.

BIBLIOGRAPHY

1. Bible Knowledge Commentary, Cook Communication Ministries, 1983, 2000
2. Elmer Towns, The Ultimate Guide to the Names of God, BethanyHouse, 2014, p.222
3. Haruna B. Goroh, Supporting your Pastor, Sure Destiny, 2016
4. https://www.livescience.com/2178-what-is-culture-defination-of-culture.html
5. Jim Muncy, Time Basics, James A Muncy, 2014, p.65
6. LT Devega and Christine Ortega Guarkee, All you want to know but didn't think you could ask, Struit Christian Books, 2012, p.120
7. Neil T. Anderson, Renewing your mind, BethanyHouse, 2014, p.46
8. The Biblical Illustrator, Ages Software Inc. and Biblesoft Inc., 2002, 2003, 2006